Big Bad Bodie: High Sierra Ghost Town

by

James Watson

and

Doug Brodie

Robert D. Reed Publishers • San Francisco, CA

Robert D. Reed Publishers
750 La Playa Street, Suite 647
San Francisco, CA 94121
Phone: 650/994-6570 • Fax: -6579
E-mail: 4bobreed@msn.com
www.rdrpublishers.com

Book Design by Marilyn Yasmine Nadel

ISBN: 1-931741-10-7
Library of Congress Card Number: 00-192299
Produced and Printed in the United States of America

CONTENTS

ACKNOWLEDGMENTS

The authors wish to acknowledge the following persons and organizations for their very kind assistance in providing information and/or photographs for inclusion in this publication. Without their aid the authors would have been unable to produce this book. The late Mrs. Anna Alena DeChambeau McKenzie...Joan Little Remington...Moss Little Pickering... the late Mrs. Ruth Little...Mono County Courthouse...Mono County Museum...the late Mrs. Anne Morres...Ross Morres...Stewart Indian Museum, Carson City, Nevada...California State Park Rangers Assn....Mark L. Whitehead....Bodie Consolidated Mining Co....Catherine Mathisen....the late George Hoeper and Alice Hoeper...the late Kent DeChambeau and Dolly DeChambeau...Kent Pierce...the Friends of Bodie....Allen (Cindy) O'Connor...California State Library...Daniel Bryant...Brad Sturdevant...Dorothy Rollins...Arlene Reveal and Staff of Mono County Library...Bill Mitchell, Administrator of Eastern California Museum of Inyo County and staff, Independence, California...Sally Gaines, Artemisia Press of Lee Vining, California...Diana Watson...Dean Watson for map assistance...Frank D. and Joan Millslagle...Wanda Biggs...John Holt...Thelma Roebuck...Mark Hunter of the Alamosa (Colorado) Valley Courier...Laura Brown...Muriel McMurtrey...George Groth...the late Mrs. Loretta Gray...Mrs. Ferne Tracey...Department of Museums, Library and Arts, Nevada State Library and Archives...Steve Scarboro....Al Avery...Inyo Register/ Chalfant Press.

INTRODUCTION

During the years 1879 through 1881, Bodie, California was considered to be one of the richest mining towns in the West. Some believed it could have been again.

As a "ghost town" today, Bodie is located at an altitude of 8,369 feet in the Sierra Nevada Mountains near the Nevada border. It is a California historic state park comprising 1,128 acres, 20 miles southeast of Bridgeport, California via US Highway 395. State Route 270 then extends 13 miles east of 395 with the final three miles unpaved packed gravel, usually inaccessible in winter, except by snowmobile.

Bodie reached a population of 10,000 during its heyday and earned a reputation as the roughest, toughest most lawless mining camp in the West. Over its lifetime, Bodie's gold and silver production topped 100 million dollars, based upon today's prices. The 175 buildings that stand following a disastrous 1932 fire are maintained by the State of California in a condition described as "arrested decay;" they will never be restored, but are prevented from further deterioration through a system of constant repair.

The park is kept open year-round, but is best visited during the summer. At other times weather is unpredictable. A vehicle fee is charged those visiting the park. Visitors wishing to pass through pay no fee.

Bodie is the best-preserved ghost town in the West. Because it continues to thrive, some of its mysterious past—its "ghosts"—remain to haunt the old buildings and diggings. This book is a compilation of tales and descriptions from the yesteryears. Included is historical lore, and many items and facts never before told about the town and as such, may allow old Bill Bodey, the town's namesake, wherever he may be, to finally rest in peace.

Compiled in print for the first time are facts about the mysterious little boy who started that fire in 1932 which burned down half the town.

He's long been known only as: "Bodie Bill." The circumstances and his true identity are revealed.

Answers are provided to such questions as: Who is buried in the grave of the town's namesake, William S. Bodey? Why is "BODIE" not spelled "BODEY" after old "William S.? (Or was it?) What is Bodie's suburb? What was Bodie's scourge? Why didn't the town have more than one railroad? What is a "horse snowshoe?" Is there still gold in them thar hills?

Highlighted are photographs depicting not only Bodie's past, but many glimpses of the town today taken by co-author Jim Watson.

Bodie's tough reputation was deserved. Its residents had to be rugged to survive even one winter. And the old phrase, "Gold is where you find it," described the community's location which evolved due to the discovery of gold. It was a site not selected for its beauty, convenience, or close proximity to any decent mode of transportation. The town "growed like Topsy," and not a tree sought the light of day in that harsh alkaline soil. Hardly a bush, other than sagebrush, offered protection from the elements. It was found that hops would grow, but little else. Trees were tried, and they died. But this didn't deter prospectors, because this was where the gold was.

Holes dug in the ground crudely covered with branches, hides, old blankets and turf served as the first dwellings. Building materials were difficult to come by, and were expensive. In time, tents dotted the landscape and a few wood structures popped up. Tired old buildings that still stood in nearby Aurora, earlier known as Esmeralda, were gradually dismantled and the timbers and bricks hauled by wagon to be re-erected in Bodie.

Bodie became a melting pot. Its citizens represented the world. Some of the names that make the old town a familiar place include Mark Twain (who was active in Aurora, but may not have ever visited Bodie), Leland Stanford, H.M. Yerington, J.S. Cain, Theodore Hoover and his famous President brother, Herbert Hoover, and many others.

Bodie's boom period was short-lived and the town settled back to a slower pace after some four peak years. Other such boom towns still exist, but not as "ghost" towns. Rather today they remain small communities with place names such as Tonopah, Sonora, Placerville (Hang Town), Mariposa, Angels Camp, Auburn and Coulterville. Many others, such as Aurora, Dogtown and Jackass Hill just disappeared after the mines petered out.

Bodie is unique in history. It remains. And in that "state of arrested decay," it is as it was many years ago. Gold was discovered in the Bodie area in 1859 by the town's namesake, but the community did not reach its zenith until 20 years later. Its rapid growth extended from 1877 through 1881. Then a gradual decline set in and by 1935 the place was all but deserted. The situation wasn't helped by the 1932 fire, but enough structures still exist to make a visit very worthwhile and educational, especially for the younger set. The kids love it!

Only a private watchman, Martin Gianettoni, lived in this treasure of the past when it was established as a state park in 1962. He had done his best to prevent looters from destroying the deserted old town. And because of his efforts, the Bodie seen today was the Bodie he saved. It appears much as it did over 60 years ago when the last permanent residents departed.

Prior to purchase of the town by the State of California, Bodie was owned by the Cain Family—descendants of James Stuart Cain. He had foreseen a future for Bodie back in the 1880s, 1890s and on into the early 1900s, even when most others thought of Bodie as dead and gone. J.S. Cain purchased buildings and property as, one by one, Bodieites sold out and moved away—and only J.S. Cain was buying. He steadfastly believed the town would again prosper—that a large tonnage of workable ore in the mine dumps and in surface mining in his Standard Mine property could be treated at a profit. His heirs, continuing as the "J.S. Cain Co.," abided by his wishes and maintained his properties.

Through their efforts Bodie continued to exist and they paid the caretaker to patrol the property for several years before and after mining operations were halted due to restrictions established during World War II.

Governor Goodwin J. Knight, in 1956, signed an appropriations bill passed by the California State Legislature authorizing the purchase of Bodie and in June, 1962, the first state park ranger arrived to direct protection of the town and property. Dedication ceremonies establishing Bodie as a State Historical Landmark and a National Historical Site were held Sept. 12, 1964.

The Bodie of today has no commercial facilities. Items for sale consist only of publications based upon Bodie and film. Everything in the park is of historical significance and nothing may be collected or removed by state law. Metal detectors are forbidden and, for the protection of the public, certain unstable sections of the park are posted as prohibited areas. These are closed to entry by park visitors, unless by special tour.

A self-guiding brochure describing a brief history of each park building is available at the park office or by mail. A museum is open from Memorial Day weekend through Labor Day weekend, 10 a.m. to 5 p.m.

The museum originally was built by the early-day minors. It was dedicated in December, 1877, as the Miners Union Hall; and served as the center of Bodie social activities for many years. It fell into disuse about 1900 and stood abandoned until the summer of 1943 when Victor Cain, son of old J.S. Cain, and Victor's wife, Ella, leased it and turned it into a museum. They ran into a problem when it was discovered the floor had been hung on springs for dancing. Vibrations which once had tickled the toes of early-day party-goers, were now causing fragile showpieces to vibrate and fall to the floor. They had the springs removed and the museum has been in use ever since.

The Cains also are responsible for saving Bodie's Methodist Church. In the summer of 1943 the sum of $100 was needed to prevent a foreclosure sale. The Cains prevailed upon the Chinese owner of the town's only saloon, Sam Leon, to host a dance in his establishment with funds derived to save the church. A total of $65 was raised, and the remaining $35 was gathered up in donations. The church remains a highlight in Bodie.

In the mid 1990s there appeared a possibility that gold mining might return to the Bodie scene when a major mining firm established plans to develop an open pit gold mine to extract ore from the ridge up behind the town—behind Bodie Bluff and Standard Hill. The company proposed gold recovery through conventional milling and CIP (carbon in pulp) processing for high grade ore and by heap leach (cyanide) processing for the larger tonnages of low grade ore.

The profit potential for the mining conglomerate would have run into the billions of dollars and the final chapter of this book explains the proposal and what happened to it.

Enjoy

J. W. and D.W.B.

'BODIE'

She's just and old town named Bodie
And ghosts now walk the streets.
Tucked in the middle of nowhere,
Where cobwebs and tumbleweeds meet.

There are sounds in haunting whispers,
Spirits of yore gossip and chat,
A broken chair lies there in pieces
Where some old timer once sat.

There were miners seeking their fortunes,
Gold was there just to be seized.
While back breaking work of hauling in wood
Was done by imported Chinese.

Of course, there was popular Rosa May,
Pleasing men of lust and sin.
In this naughty town by the name of Bodie
In the midst of the noise and din.

The devil saw all the ruckus
And decided to make a kill.
By fire, destroyed the town of Bodie
Sparked off by Bodie Bill.

There was the end of Bodie
But we know they're still there as of old,
The Chinese still hauling the wood in,
The miners still searching for gold.

The spirits are haunting and active.
There is still plenty of shooting and fights.
Bodie Bill is still playing with matches,
While Rosa May is quite busy at night.

By Dorothy Rollins

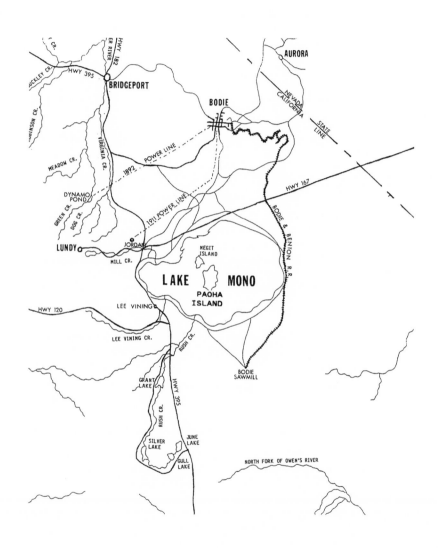

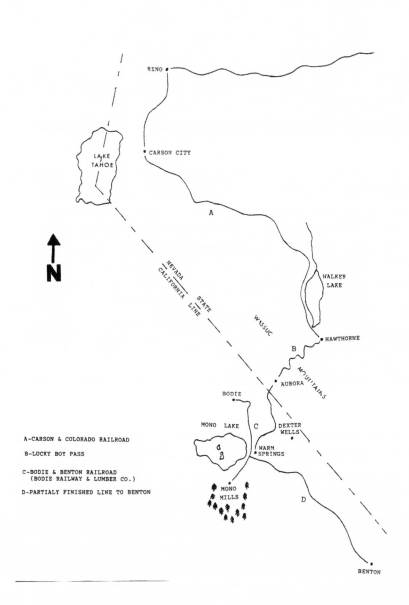

RENO

LAKE TAHOE

CARSON CITY

A

NEVADA
CALIFORNIA STATE LINE

WASSUC

WALKER LAKE

HAWTHORNE

B

MOUNTAINS

AURORA

BODIE

MONO LAKE

C

DEXTER WELLS

WARM SPRINGS

MONO MILLS

D

BENTON

N

A-CARSON & COLORADO RAILROAD

B-LUCKY BOY PASS

C-BODIE & BENTON RAILROAD
(BODIE RAILWAY & LUMBER CO.)

D-PARTIALY FINISHED LINE TO BENTON

CHAPTER 1

THE MAN, BODEY

W.S. Bodey
William S. Bodey
Waterman S. Bodey
Wakeman S. Bodey
William Smith Bodie

The historian has a choice of determining the namesake of the historic gold mining town of Bodie, California. It is generally assumed the town derived its name following the 1859 death of William S. Bodey, and the spelling variation is itself a story, and generally assumed to be a mistake, albeit purposeful, on the part of a sign painter.

The spelling of the surname has even occasionally been spelled "Body," and the mining district named after him as "Boda."

Immortality on the part of Mr. Bodey was derived from the discovery of gold near the site of the town later named in his honor. And the discovery actually wasn't his alone. He was one of a five-member prospecting party consisting of himself, William Boyle, Pat Garraty, Terrence Brodigan and E. S. "Black" Taylor. Taylor was part Cherokee Indian and was dark skinned, hence his nickname. The five prospectors had traversed the Sierra Nevada Mountains during the summer of 1859 from Sonora in Tuolumne County, California, seeking gold, working their way north from Mono Lake to near Aurora in country that had seen few white men and was frequented by several Indian tribes. Due to the Indian threat, the group headed back, reaching the area known as Silver Hill, above and southeast of what is now the town of Bodie. It is south of Bodie Bluff.

They discovered gold in a small ravine called Rattlesnake Gulch. Geologists later determined that the ore they found actually had "spilled" down the ravine from rich deposits higher up on the bluff. However, it was gold, and it was just what the group was searching for.

Winter was approaching. The prospectors split up, planning to return in the spring. There were reports the five pledged secrecy as to the find and that Bodey broke that pledge, but no proof of this exists. Bodey and Taylor decided to remain near the discovery site for the winter and erected a small cabin in an area they christened "Taylor Gulch" after Black Taylor. It was during a return trip to the cabin from the town of Monoville in a November, 1859 blizzard, that the untimely death of Bodey occurred. Bodey died at the age of 45.

The pair had loaded themselves down with supplies when the deepening snow made their progress almost impossible and Bodey collapsed on the trail. Unable to carry his partner, Taylor wrapped Bodey in a blanket and propped him up against a tree, vowing to return for him as soon as he was able to reach the cabin and deposit the supplies. After a brief rest in the cabin, Taylor returned to the trail in search of his partner, but to no avail. Bodie was buried somewhere beneath an ever-deepening blanket of snow and it wasn't until the following March of 1860 that Taylor and a companion, Johnson King, found their friend's skeletal remains.

Animals had attacked the body. Bones were scattered. One arm was missing. Dejectedly the two men placed Bodey's remains in the weathered blanket in which Taylor had wrapped him and buried Bodey in a shallow grave. In fitting remembrance, the two men pointed Bodey's feet toward the promontory later named "Bodie Bluff." They placed a large boulder at the head of the grave as a marker.

There, Bodey lay interred for 20 years. He was not forgotten, however, and the nearby town and surrounding mining district that developed during the following years were named in his honor.

In Mark Twain's book "Roughing It," is his description of a similar event in which he and two friends, Mr. Ballou and a Prussian named Ollendorff, on horseback, rode for two or three days through a snowstorm en route to Carson City to investigate the many assessments placed upon mine holdings belonging to Twain and his brother, Orion.

Ollendorf boasted that his senses were "…as dead certain as a compass," and led the group through the snow for hours, until they eventually realized they were following their own tracks. By this time they were hopelessly lost after traveling in circles and then attempting to light a fire, first by twice firing a bullet into a pile of twigs; then, after discovering four matches in a pocket, igniting each unsuccessfully. They prepared to die on the trail and each tearfully lamented his evil way of life. Ollendorf gave up liquor; Ballou threw away his old and greasy pack of cards.

Twain wrote: "We were all sincere, and all deeply moved and earnest, for we were in the presence of death and without hope.

"I threw away my pipe, and in doing it felt that at last I was free of a hated vice and one that had ridden me like a tyrant all my days.... We put our arms about each other's necks and awaited the warning drowsiness that precedes death by freezing."

The three had even lost their horses when Twain, who was supposed to hold the bridles… "unconsciously dropped them and the released animals had walked off in the storm."

The three men became immobile and covered with snow when Twain became aware that he was apparently still alive. "This is death - this is the hereafter," he wrote. "Then came a white upheaval at my side, and a voice said, with bitterness:

"'Will some gentleman be so good as to kick me behind?'

"It was Ballou-at least it was a towzled snow image in a sitting posture, with Ballou's voice," and Twain rose up, "and in the gray dawn, not fifteen steps from us, were the frame buildings of a stage station, and under a shed stood our still saddled and bridled horses!

"I have scarcely exaggerated a detail of this curious and absurd adventure. It occurred almost exactly as I have stated it. We actually went into camp in a snow-drift in a desert, at midnight in a storm, forlorn and hopeless, within fifteen steps of a comfortable inn."[1]

Bodey's gravesite was discovered in 1879, two decades after his death, by Bodie judge and later Nevada State Senator J. G. McClinton, who, after enlisting the aid of his closest friend, the Hon. Joseph Wasson, with other Bodie community leaders, exhumed the remains.

A description of the exhumation in the Mammoth City Times, a publication issued in the nearby community of Mammoth City but printed on presses in Bodie, stated:

"The work commenced about half past 11 a.m. and in about three fourths of an hour a much decomposed silk necktie was unearthed. Soon followed a pretty well preserved shoe, attached to the right foot of all that is left of W. S. Bodey. The heel of the shoe is much worn or broken down as to the upper leather, as if it has been used more as a slipper. The bones of the feet were found quite disjointed, and the shoe of the left foot missing entirely, the foot having been apparently wrapped in some sort of cloth... some of the clothing and the blanket before mentioned were found pretty well preserved, the most perfect relic thus far obtained was the necktie, which was probably removed by the burial party and tossed upon the feet of the corpse. Even this relic is interwoven with roots of sagebrush.

"... The skull was well preserved, the teeth being in a perfect state of preservation. About the waist was found a belt with a leather scabbard and knife attached... Warren Loose was digging and exclaimed: 'Here's his knife; I've heard Brodigan say he always wore it.' The hilt of the knife is marked with a medallion of a woman's head on one side and a lion on the other. The scabbard is evidently a home made affair, fastened by bullet rivets."[2]

The two men who had buried Bodey 20 years earlier were not around when the remains were found. Johnson King had long since disappeared and Black Taylor reportedly wandered first to Monoville, then to Dog Town (the remains are located at the west edge of the Highway 395/State Route 270 turnoff to Bodie) and finally to the nearby town of Benton. He fought with hostile Piute Indians, was killed and it was said he was decapitated and that his head was "passed around and observed in several locations."

After Bodey's remains were exhumed and taken into town, the citizens were informed by the Pacific Coast Pioneer Society, an organization established early on to compile Bodie's history, that Bodey's remains would be reinterred November 2, 1879, in the Bodie Cemetery with the society handling arrangements. All businesses were requested to close, with bells to be tolled during ceremonies and flags to be hung at half-staff.

At this point it would have seemed fitting that Bodey's remains be suitably interred in the cemetery with a simple headstone and allowed to remain. But this was not to be.

The Hon. R.D. Ferguson of the Pioneers delivered a laudatory eulogy. He referred to Bodey as "A man of indomitable pluck and energy," adding that "it would be a pleasing thought if we could imagine that his generous spirit, freed from its ancient prison-house of clay, was still prospecting in that undiscovered country on the other side of the great river."

Ferguson further proclaimed: "Let a fit and enduring monument be reared in his memory. Let its base be wrought from the chiseled granite of these mountains. Let a marble shaft rise high above with sculptured urn o'ertopping, with the simple name of Bodey there, to kiss the first golden rays of the coming sun, and where its setting beams may linger in cloudless majesty and beauty, undisturbed forever."

He concluded: "And so we leave poor Bodey with his God alone."[3]

The eulogist's words were heartily endorsed by Bodie's citizens and, in the November 22, 1879 issue of the Bodie Chronicle, appeared this notice:

"BODEY'S MONUMENT. Proposals have been received from Wells Kirkpatrick of the Bodie Foundry to furnish a cast iron monument to be erected in the memory of Bodey. The Pioneers will act upon the proposition next Tuesday evening." [4]

Apparently the plan for a cast iron monument was dropped in favor of the granite edifice as described by Ferguson in his eulogy and the goodly sum of $500 was quickly subscribed to by Bodie townspeople. Late in 1880 a sculptor from San Francisco was summoned to fashion from native granite a "marble shaft" complete with "sculptured urn o'ertopping with the simple name of..."

At this point there was a departure from the original text. As the sculptor was about to chisel "BODEY" in the granite base of the 12-foot-high monument, the Nation's 20th President, James A. Garfield, was felled by an assassin's bullet. He lingered but died September 19, 1881. When this news reached Bodie the citizens decided their priorities tended to favor their late President. The monument was completed and the monolith stands to this day, towering above all others in the cemetery.

TALLEST MONUMENT: This Bodie Cemetery monolith, 12-feet high,
was fashioned by a San Francisco sculptor hired by the citizens to
honor William S. Bodey. Today's visitor to Bodie will be surprised
at the name chiseled into its base. (A Jim Watson photo)

It honors, not William S. Bodey. The inscription chiseled into granite
reads:

TO THE MEMORY OF JAMES A GARFIELD
PRS. OF U.S.
SEPT. 19, 1881
ERECTED JAN. 1882

Somewhere, further up the hill (no one knows exactly where), in an unmarked grave overgrown with sagebrush and weeds, lie the remains of the town's namesake, the man the community forgot—forgot to provide a replacement for that marble shaft—even forgot where the grave is located and almost forgot how to spell his name!

As for President Garfield, that cold January day in 1882 the schools and businesses in Bodie and even in surrounding communities were closed. Everyone journeyed to Bodie where solemn funeral services were held for the late President. An empty casket was carried from downtown to the cemetery in a procession. Dr. J.W. Van Zandt delivered the oration. Buildings were draped in mourning.

Newspaper accounts noted the procession began at the Miners Union Hall and the casket was placed upon a bier, which was covered with a black velvet pall with heavy silver fringe. On the casket was a silver plate upon which were engraved the words: "James A. Garfield, died September 19, 1881, aged 50 years." At the head and foot were monuments of flowers and in the center a large white wreath.[5]

The empty casket, representing Mono County's grief, was interred in the Bodie Cemetery. It is above this empty "grave" that the granite monument stands as a shrine for President Garfield.

There is a strong suspicion that wherever William S. Bodey is buried, his remains will forever be in question, for not everyone was convinced in 1879 that the body found in that old unmarked grave was that of Bodey. For instance, the Mammoth City Times printed a story November 8 of that year that cast doubt on the matter.

"The Bodieites in an Agony of Doubt, But Determined That Their Late 'Find' Shall be Bodey's Body anyhow. A ghastly state of doubt and uncertainty has seized upon the minds of Bodieites. The other day Judge McClinton and Jos. Wasson went out and found a skeleton, which they at once proclaimed to be the body of W.S. Bodey. The newspapers jumping at the same conclusion, published column after column of reminiscences of the deceased, his virtues, etc., etc. Then came the Pioneers and they removed the skeleton, interred it in the Bodie Cemetery with distinguished honors and went about the erection of a costly monument. Up to this time no body had dared murmur a doubt as to the genuinness of Judge McClinton's find, though a good many thought it a great pity that the remains could not be positively identified.

"But now comes one James Hunt, who knew Bodey well in life, and was with him just before his death, and says the Wasson-McClinton skeleton is not Bodey's at all, but some one else's. In a card to the newspaper, Hunt says:

"'I laughed all over my face when I read that with the remains they found a Bowie knife ten inches long and a shoe still containing the bones of a foot. The fact is that during my acquaintance with Mr. Bodie the only knife he carried was a pocket knife, with a spoon and fork attached, and he always wore old stogy boots'."

The newspaper story continues: "This statement of Hunt's has thrown the whole of Bodie into a paroxysm of rage. The papers howl at him, one calls him a 'pestilent fellow' and a 'transparent fraud' and another dubs him 'an infamous liar'. We are inclined to believe that Mr. Hunt is right, and that the Bodieites believe it now themselves; but have had their ceremonial services, their graphic descriptions, their eloquent addresses and all that, they don't intend to give up to the outside world that they have been fooled. But we don't believe the monument will be built."

The newspaper was prophetic without realizing it. It was half right. Of course the monument was sculpted, but as it turned out, not for Bodie but rather for the late President Garfield. And, perhaps Mr. Hunt's reference to the skeletal remains containing a "pretty well preserved shoe... much worn or broken down as to the upper leather, as if it had been used more as a slipper" is more to the point than originally thought, for why would a man wear slipper-type shoes while on the trail to obtain supplies some distance away, and in November when it would be cold and likely to snow, as it did? Would he not be more likely to wear "old stogy boots?"[6]

The Mammoth City Times the following week carried a story headed: "NOT BODY'S BONES." It stated: "The 'bones of Body' over which so much fuss was lately made in Bodie, proved to be the bones of some other fellow," and, in the same edition, is an editorial poking fun at the town:

"The finding of Body's bones and their subsequent interment in Bodie with reverential ceremony, is regarded in this arctic latitude as the grimmest joke that that grim humorist, the Hon. Joseph Wasson, ever perpetrated. How gets on the monument, Joseph? Don't let it meet the same fate that the Tweed Monument met in New York."

The newspaper was humorously comparing Wasson's statements

about Bodie with the then-infamous politician William Marcy "Boss" Tweed of New York City, who died in prison in 1878 after being convicted of fraud.

Not only was Wasson a leading Bodie citizen, he was an author and later a Nevada State Senator from the Fourth District, certainly not one to be ridiculed, but newspapers in those days enjoyed hurling barbs at each other and at noted personages.

Another unverified story made the rounds that Taylor did not find his partner's body on the trail the following spring of 1860, but that a search party looking for the lost prospector, actually found it and transported it to Aurora and where it was buried in the Aurora Cemetery. This report supposedly was substantiated by Josiah Kirlew, a prospector who had worked the general area in 1860. No one paid heed to Kirlew's tale, however, and Taylor was unavailable for questioning. Certainly, no member of a search party, if it ever existed, reported such an incident. And no gravestone was ever found in the Aurora Cemetery bearing the name "William S. Bodey."

HOW "BODEY" BECAME "BODIE"

Judge McClinton is credited with the story of how the town received its misspelled name and the identity of the man responsible. In a letter to the Bodie Standard in 1879 he explained the misspelling was due to the action of a sign painter whom he identified as Robert W. Howland, of Aurora and Bodie. He wrote that Professor J.E. Clayton and the Haslett brothers, Ben and John, who owned a hay ranch located between the two towns, verbally ordered Howland to paint "BODEY STABLE" on a sign to be erected on their ranch building. They were absent when Howland executed their order, and did not know he took poetic license and intentionally misspelled "BODEY" because he liked "BODIE."

The sign read "BODIE STABLE" when completed and area residents favored the new spelling so it was decided to leave it as "BODIE."

Judge McClinton concluded: "I am not now certain to whom we are indebted for the orthagraphical improvement, but I think it was Robert W. Howland who is now in Bodie, and at any rate, Bob was the first sign painter I remember having seen in Aurora."[7]

Howland was described as being "a friend and cabin mate of Mark Twain" by author Warren Loose. Twain resided in an around Aurora in the early 1860s when the town was first known as "Esmeralda." Loose, like Judge McClinton, also credits Howland with the misspelling of Bodie after 1937 interviews with two early-day Bodieites, John Parr, in Piedmont, California, and W.H. "Billy" Metson in San Francisco. Both men were in their eighties at the time of the interviews and both described sign-painter Howland as "the man who publicly changed the spelling of Bodey's name."

WHAT KIND OF MAN?

William S. Bodey was an enigma; a man of many faces, at least at the time of his reinterrment it appeared he was, judging from the various descriptions of the man and his family.

The Bodie Chronicle, November 1, 1879:

"Sylvanus B. Cobb of this city informs us that he was a partner of the deceased pioneer from the fall of 1857 until the early part of 1859, and that his name was William S. BODEY—not BODY—and that he was a very fine man, temperate in his habits and very neat in his personal appearance, in fact, uncommonly so. He was 5 feet 6 inches in height, light complexioned, with hair and whiskers very gray, and aged about 45 years. Mr. Bodey's family to which he was much attached, resided in Poughkeepsie, New York, where he had a daughter, aged 19 years, graduate, and a boy, 17 years of age, was preparing to enter college. Mr. Cobb was Bodey's partner until he started for Bodie and he says he would never wish to have a better man for a partner."[8]

Cobb's description of Bodey's family differs markedly from that of Helen Myers who wrote an article on William S. Bodey in 1961 for the Poughkeepsie Journal, a newspaper in Bodey's native town. Mrs. Myers wrote that Bodey's wife's name was Sarah, but that the couple had two sons, Ogden and George, all of whom he left in Poughkeepsie when he sailed for San Francisco in 1849 to seek gold. [9]

Two more authors, Roger D. McGrath and Frank S. Wedertz, both state Bodey was a native of New York State and that prior to his journey west he worked as a tinsmith in Poughkeepsie. Writes McGrath: "He caught the gold fever in 1848. Leaving behind a wife and six children, he booked passage on the Matthew Vassar .. he spent the next ten years working the placer deposits of the Mother Lode. Although he never had more than modest success, he was able to send money home regularly to support his wife and children..."[10]

Wedertz writes: "He wrote regularly to his wife and sent money for the support of their six children. Bodey's wife remained in Poughkeepsie where she made a meager living as a seamstress. One by one her six children died, thus adding a last tragic note surrounding the curse that followed the discoverers."[11] Wedertz's reference to a "curse" must have been based upon the untimely deaths of Bodey, Black Taylor, and the others who made up the original group of prospectors.

Another bit of mystery is added when the great-grandniece of one William Smith Bodie arrived in California from Elgin, Scotland in 1969. Her family records suggest William Smith Bodie may be the actual discoverer of the Bodie District. She stated his name was always spelled with the -IE and that he left his native Buckie, Scotland on a family ship. Wedertz notes that a letter written by William Smith Bodie from Monoville would appear to be strong evidence that he is the town's namesake, and his Scottish brogue would explain why some of his early acquaintances thought he was Dutch as the accents are similar. After receiving several letters from him, the family lost touch with him. This, of course, could have been about the time he perished in the blizzard.[12]

So, what was William S. Bodey really like (if that is his real name)?

In the November 3, 1879 Bodie Daily Free Press, an old timer attending Bodey's disinterrment stated: "I knew Bodey intimately for two years and he never drank a drop."[13] And yet another man, Frank Shaw, who said he knew Bodey in Monoville, described him as "The dirtiest man I ever met."[14]

And so, the enigma exists and, so far as can be determined, the remains of William S. Bodey are interred somewhere on the hillside where the Bodie Cemetery is located. The seriousness of the situation was made light of in the Mammoth City Times in an editorial:

"GRAVELY THUS—Some one left the gate of the cemetery open last night, and he let in a terrific draft of cold air. It was so cold that Bill Bodey got up and shut the gate with such a slam that both hinges were broken off. The residents of that section state that his language on that occasion was frightful."[15]

Following this, the Gold Hills News wrote:

"The Free Press is given to joking on grave subjects. The Press should bear in mind, however, that Bodey has only his bones with him, therefore was at a disadvantage as compared with the army of pneumoniacs which have been so rapidly gathered in there of late. The idea of the skeletonian old prospector being thus installed as gate keeper and superintendent of the Bodie Boneyard is perfectly appropriate and good."[16]

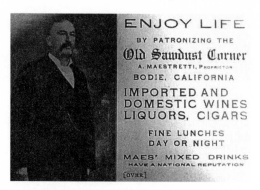

This business card bears the photo of the owner of the Old Sawdust
Corner Saloon. The tavern was the location of the start of the 1932
Bodie Fire. (A Jim Watson photo)

FOOTNOTES — CHAPTER 1

1. Mark Twain, "Roughing It," Pages 213-222
2. Mammoth City Times, November 8, 1879
3. Bodie Chronicle, November 8, 1879
4. Ibid, November 22, 1879
5. Mammoth City Times, November 8, 1879
6. Bodie Standard, October 7, 1879
7. Ibid, November 15, 1879
8. Bodie Chronicle, November 1, 1879
9. Poughkeepsie Journal article by Mrs. Helen Meyers, February 5, 1961
10. Roger D. McGrath, "Gunfighters Highwaymen and Vigilantes," Page 102
11. Frank S. Wedertz, "Bodie 1859-1900," Pages 3, 203
12. Ibid
13. Bodie Daily Free Press, November 3, 1879
14. Ibid, November 3, 1879
15. Mammoth City Times, November 8, 1879
16. Gold Hill News, November 15, 1879

CHAPTER 2

LET'S GO TO SCHOOL IN BODIE

Obtaining an education in an obscure, isolated mining town called "Bodie" was a challenge in mid and late nineteenth century America. It was especially challenging when it came to attending the "Highest School in California." Four elementary schools existed in Mono County at the start of Bodie's glory days of 1877 and 1878. They were Bridgeport, Antelope, Benton and North Antelope. The first mention of a Bodie school was an item in the 1877–1878 Common School Report submitted by Mono County Superintendent of Schools W.T. Elliott to the California State Superintendent of Public Instruction.

Elliott informed the state official that "the schools of Mono County are in a prosperous condition and have for the past year been under the charge of competent teachers. Two new districts have been organized and in one of them, Bodie, a move is already made toward voting a tax to build a commodious school house. The schools are well supplied, or most of them, with modern furniture, but are wanting in apparatus. There are now six schools in the county (he did not name the additional one) which are located in communities separated from each other by barren wastes, which render it difficult to reach them, except at a considerable outlay of expense. The people are generally quite interested in the welfare of the schools and education holds a high rank in their opinions.

"Bodie is a new mining town rapidly assuming a position of importance, but at present has poor accommodations for their school in a building occupied, and it is hoped they will soon secure rooms suited to their needs."[1]

The Bodie Public School opened its doors the second Tuesday of March, 1878. The first teacher, according to Everett O'Rourke, author of "The Highest School in California," was Miss Belle Moore, who greeted ten students, all eager to begin their education, in the Cary Building on South Main Street. By the end of the second week, a total of 40 students were crowded into the one-room facility and after three months, when the end of the term arrived, enrollment had skyrocketed to 76, with pupils ranging in age from five to big 17-year-old boys with beards.

The teacher received a salary of $100.00 per month. Because of the rapidly increasing student load, the special school tax was levied in the fall to finance construction of a school building on Green Street. It was completed in January, 1879, "complete with a cupola."[2]

Whether O'Rourke was correct in his identification of the first teacher as Belle Moore, or whether Loose in his book, "Bodie Bonanza," was correct when he identified her as "Miss Nelly Donnally," or whether she actually was "Mrs. Annie Donnelly," as stated in other sources, cannot be determined.

Loose wrote, "In mid-March (1878) an inquiring reporter paid a visit to Bodie's first school. Miss Nelly Donnally was the teacher of some 14 bright-eyed pupils attending classes in the new Cary Building on South Main Street. Miss Donnally expressed hope more parents in Bodie would send their children to school and indicated children at home outnumbered those in attendance."[3]

Annie Donnelly's identity was mentioned in the January 9, 1878 issue of the Bodie Standard, which noted that early that month the first term of the first public school in Bodie commenced "in the home of Annie Donnelly;" that the class size was 14, and that she appealed to parents to send their children to school. As a result, the newspaper reported, enrollment had increased until her home could no longer accommodate the students and a summer term was postponed because no school facility could be found to handle the student load.

The Standard story: "Classroom space was eventually leased in the Cary Building on Main Street and a special tax was levied to provide funds for the construction of a schoolhouse. By late February, 1879, a schoolhouse 'complete with cupola' had been erected on Green Street and the teachers were expecting to greet some eighty students for the spring term."[4]

Although a new structure, the school was not equipped with bathroom facilities, was poorly ventilated, and had few items of furniture, but the superintendent reported, "the district does use the entire service of State textbooks." Bodie came of age politically during this period when the school district was established November 6, 1877; the Bodie Road District, February 5, 1877, and the Bodie Township November 6, 1878.

Early in 1878 Bodie's population topped 1,200 with 175 to 180 cabins and dwellings; several saloons; six restaurants and three general stores. Ironically, 175 is the number of structures remaining in Bodie today. The Town's rapid growth was noted in the superintendent's 1878–1879 report:

LODGING HOUSE TO SCHOOL:
The original Bodie School burned down and was replaced in 1879
by this structure, the Bon Ton Lodging House, which was moved two
blocks to its present location on Green Street. (A Jim Watson photo)

"There are, with one exception, Bodie, provided with sufficient room to accommodate all the children. Nearly all have the improved seats. Bodie built at quite an expense a new school house, but by the rapid growth of the place they now have scarce room to accommodate one-half of the children of school age. They will build a new building as soon as the trustees can raise the money, through the usual method of voting a tax, which will no doubt be easily accomplished judging by the interest, general among the people there in the cause of education."[5]

The space problem was solved as the result of an arson incident. The first bond issue built the first school in 1879 on Green Street, but it burned down shortly after construction. The blaze occurred during a fight between several students, some larger than one of the teachers, a Mr.

Cook, who even had his beard pulled during the scuffling. He remained on the job until he was replaced at year's end by a Mr. McCarty who proved to be a man of strength and "with the aid of a black iron poker," battled the 17 and 18 year old toughs to a standstill, regaining order in the classroom. One by one, the troublemakers quit school and order was restored.

Bodie needed a replacement school to resume classes in the 1879 school year and so the Bon Ton Lodging House was called into service. The town fathers built a belfry atop the structure and it was moved two blocks from its original site on Main Street to the site it presently occupies on Green Street. This was the site the burned structure occupied and the "Bon Ton" school can be seen today, one of the buildings that escaped the disastrous Bodie fire of 1932.

The Bon Ton had been located just three doors down from the old Bodie Standard Newspaper office, which operated from a two-story building at the corner of Main and King Streets.

When a building was moved in those days it was usually during the winter when the ground was frozen. Logs were placed under the structure and it was simply "rolled" along the frozen road, pulled by horses and mules. Fortunately, the Bon Ton had been available for sale and was large enough to handle the growth of the student population.

Bodie's bonanza period continued through 1880. "People flocked into town almost as rapidly as summer tourists do today. The county superintendent reported there were three schools in the district and that 615 students were enrolled... residents of the district had voted a tax of 16 cents per $100 of assessed valuation and cash paid for sites, buildings and furniture was $9,121.68."[6]

Times changed, however, and by 1884 some of the mines had quit producing and a delinquent tax sale that year netted over $3,000. The Clinton School District located near the Sweetwater Mountains bid on a 1-1/2 story building in Bodie to be moved and used as a school in Clinton. The purchase price was just $35!

A reference to trees in Bodie was included in O'Rourke's publication:

"One of the trustees of Bodie School District...Mr. H.C. Blanchard is having a number of pine trees transplanted to the school yard that the little ones may have shade to play in during the warm months."

This was from a report by County Superintendent Cornelia Richards in the 1900-1901 school year.[7]

Not one of the trees Mr. Blanchard had transplanted is in evidence today. In fact there is not a tree growing in Bodie. Some people who lived there say that many trees have been planted but none has survived because of the alkali in the soil. These former Bodieites do say that the only plant, foreign to Bodie, that will grow there is the hop vine.[8]

Emil W. Billeb, a resident of Bodie from 1908 to 1920, wrote in his book "Mining Camp Days":

"In Bodie we purchased the Donnelly House on the west side of town, near her (his wife) father's house (the home of James Stuart Cain). Ours was the only green spot in town. Hops covered the front and sides of our house; no other green plant could survive in Bodie's harsh climate."[9]

Alice DeChambeau, clerk of the Bridgeport Elementary School District, wrote in 1952 that the Bodie School District was suspended in 1943 for lack of pupils and lapsed into the Bridgeport District July 7, 1947.[10]

Bodie, from the period 1937 through 1939, is recalled by Kent Pierce, a resident of Stockton, California and a former Stockton-Sacramento television newsman. He and a brother, Bruce, resided with his mother, Mrs. Myrtle V. N. Pierce, during that period. Mrs. Pierce accepted the job as Bodie School teacher, moving there from the Reno area where she had taught school at Galena Creek, Nevada, on the slope of Mount Rose.

ORIGINAL LOTTIE JOHL HOME: This structure was occupied in the mid-1930s by Kent Pierce, his school-teacher mother; a brother and grandmother. The family used the front room as the Post Office, the rear room as a school, and their living quarters were in the middle. (A Jim Watson photo)

"We were at Galena Creek from 1934 through the spring of 1937. The district ran out of money and schools were consolidated, so mother grabbed the first job she could find. It was pretty slim pickings. It was a teaching job in Bodie and, of course, we said just about the same thing that little girl is quoted as saying in 1879 when she found out HER family was moving to Bodie:

"'Goodbye, God! We're going to Bodie!'

"Regardless of how we felt, we went to Bodie. If the walls of those old buildings could just talk, or if we had just had video cameras in those days…"

Pierce's mother first taught classes in 1937 in the "Bon Ton" original two-room school, using just one of the classrooms. Pierce recalls that in that first year he and his brother were joined by a cousin, Al Slattery. They were the only students.

"I can recall there were two privies. We didn't have running water—plumbing—and we always thought that was discriminatory. The girls' privy was located adjacent to the classrooms, but the boys had to walk down a windway about 40 feet. In fact, we were standing in that windway when the old transformer burned in the substation right across the street, shutting off the power."

The following year, 1938-1939, Mrs. Pierce moved to the old Lottie Johl home. Mrs. Pierce's mother, whom Kent refers to as "Gammy," joined the family and served for a short time as postmistress, with the Post Office located in the front of the dwelling. The living quarters were in the center and the rear room was used as the school classroom. After a couple of months "Gammy" moved to Santa Cruz to retire and Mrs. Pierce not only served as school teacher but she also became postmistress.

"There was still some gold extracting going on then, and mother made more money shipping gold out of the Bodie Post Office than she did as a teacher. That's because the safest and cheapest method of shipping gold at that time was by Parcel Post, and she got a commission on any Parcel Post shipments."

Pierce recalls that windfall was shortlived for his mother, however, because the winter of 1938-1939 was so severe they decided to leave Bodie, moving to Lee Vining, nearby, where his mother took a teacher substitute job. "Our car was back in Bodie. It had disappeared under snow in late October and we went back in May of 1939 and had to dig it out from under 24-foot snowdrifts. That was one of the worst winters on record in Bodie."

Pierce recalls that he and his mother and brother had arrived in Bodie just five years after the disastrous fire of June 23, 1932. Although the school closed when his mother left, it reopened in 1941 during operation of the Bodie Gilford Mining Co. which worked low-grade dump ores until late in 1942 when gold mining in the United States was halted due to World War II. Pierce recalls:

"In 1943 there were just three people left in Bodie: Sam Leon, the store and bar owner; Martin Gianettoni, a watchman for the Cain family which owned the Standard Mine, and Spence Gregory, the town handyman. When we were living in Bodie several years previously, my brother and I would go behind Sam Leon's store, pull soft drink bottles out of a case, and then run around to the front of the store and turn them in for deposit. He always paid us in candy. Then he would go out in back and put the bottles back in the case, and we would do it all over again the next day.

"In another situation, we would volunteer to clean the ashes out of Spence Gregory's pot-bellied stove because he would buy his groceries from Sam Leon and Sam always put Gregory's change in the bag with the groceries. When Gregory got home he would take the groceries out of the bag, wad the bag up and throw it into the stove. Of course, when we sifted the ashes later, out would come the change and into our pockets.

"The original telephone system was long gone by the time we moved to Bodie. When we were living there an amateur radio operator, a part-time resident, was Bodie's link to the outside. He was a ham operator and, on one occasion, I remember talking to my grandmother in Santa Cruz on his ham radio, and I'll always remember his name—Bacon."[11]

Voter registration lists indicate that the town's greatest period of growth was the year the big bonanza hit, 1879. Only men would vote so the Bodie registration list was strictly male. It crossed the gamut and of course listed a number of school teachers. Other occupations, some peculiar to the times, were: harness maker, saddle maker and wagon maker. The list also included horse trader, saloonkeeper, brick mason, miner (by the hundreds), engineer, physician, painter, blacksmith, bookkeeper, deputy sheriff, butcher, amalgamator, brewer, dentist, gambler, confectioner, restaurateur, toll road agent, capitalist, clergyman, teacher of dancing, policeman, woodsman, speculator, stock dealer, soda manufacturer and express messenger, among many others.[12]

"DOWNTOWN BODIE": This was Main Street Bodie before
the disastrous 1932 summer fire that destroyed much of the town.
(By permission of Eastern California Museum)

Truly, Bodie was the melting pot of the World. It was called a tough
town, and it had its share of undesirables, but it was amazing how well
its citizens got along together. Also amazing is how those individuals
from throughout the world found their way to that tiny community at
the top of the Sierra Nevada Mountains at the border of California and
Nevada to establish "The Highest Schools in California."

When the Bodie School opened in the fall of 1881, the Bodie Evening
Miner carried this story:

"THE BODIE PUBLIC SCHOOL—This institution reopened this
morning with Miss Ray as temporary principal, pending the arrival of a
male to assume the duties of that position. Miss Naomi Angell took
charge of the intermediate department, while Miss Jennie Bradley rules
the primary. The attendance of scholars was large. (O'Rourke listed
enrollment in 1881–1883 as 285, the highest in three years.) When the
male principal arrives Miss Ray is to have direction of the primary classes."[13]

The following day the newspaper carried this correction:

"MISS JENNIE BROPHY—The dense stupidity of a compositor
yesterday made THE MINER announce that 'Miss Jennie Bradley'
would take temporary charge of the primary department of the Bodie
Public School. The name was written, and should have been printed,

'Miss Jennie Brophy'. There is no such a young lady in Bodie, school-marm or otherwise, as Miss Jennie Bradley. The derelict compositor was very promptly and very properly discharged last night. We have no objection to the Free Press stealing our items, but we do object to that paper stealing our blunders—we have a copyright on them."(14)

The Bodie Evening Miner carried two articles on floggings in the school in August, 1881. The first, August 2:

"THE WHIPPED SCHOOL BOY—THE MINER made mention last evening of some flogging going on in the school house. At the time there was too much of both sides of the story being talked up to form anything like an unbiased opinion. It transpires that Miss Angell found it necessary to correct a lad named McQuaid, which resulted in a sensation and a town scandal. Discipline must be maintained in our pubic school; but if this boy went so far in the breach as to merit the bruised back which he exhibited last night he is beyond control in any public school.

"The public will await the action of the school trustees on this somewhat serious matter. The act of Mrs. McQuaid in wreaking vengeance on the teacher (no story appeared in the newspaper on this, but it is assumed Mrs. McQuaid must have retaliated by attacking Miss Angell) made a bad matter worse. Let an investigation quiet public scandal; and by all means let any unruly element in the public school be made to understand that discipline must and will be maintained."(15)

Six days later, on August 8, 1882, the Miner carried this follow-up story:

"THE LAST OF THE SCHOOL SCANDAL—As THE MINER at the time urged they should do, our Board of School Trustees have at last held a meeting and investigated the recent case of flogging in the school. After the necessary 'regrets' and so forth, the Board concluded their report in the following decided language: 'In no instance, however, will we countenance the interference by patrons with the duties of the teachers, advising or dictating to them the course they must pursue. We simply exact of the pupils that cheerful obedience to the rules that should be expected of them at home, and when that is refused, will be compelled to submit or withdraw from the school. (signed) Joseph J. Falkinham, T. A. Stephens, and William Davison, Trustees.'"(16)

The Miss Namoi Angell, who administered the flogging of the McQuaid boy, and apparently suffered a beating in return from the boy's mother, served as Superintendent of Mono County Schools for five years, beginning that same year, 1882 through 1887, and during those same years also served as a teacher, according to county records.

Mrs. Anne W. Morres, a resident of Carson City, Nevada when interviewed in November, 1990 by one of the authors, Doug Brodie, was in her mid-90s—she did not know her exact age since no birth records were kept in Bodie in the 1890s. Mrs. Morres died in 1991. She was of Piaute Indian origin.

Mrs. Morres and an older brother, the late Bob Wright, who also resided in Carson City, and a sister, all attended the Stewart Indian School located on a 240-acre site three miles south of Carson City in Ormsby County. The school, no longer in service, was operated by the United States Bureau of Indian Affairs.

Named after U.S. Senator William Stewart of Nevada, the school is an official historic landmark and will be preserved. During its operation it graduated over 2,800 Indian students. It was initially called "Clear Creek Indian Training School" when it opened in 1890, and also has been known variously as "Carson Indian School" and "Stewart Institute." It was closed in 1980. The school's many unique stone buildings were erected during the 1920s and 1930s, some by Indian stonemasons. The classroom building is now the Stewart Indian Museum open to the public.

The late Mrs. Ruth Little of Carson City, who taught at the school in the 1920s and was a long-time friend of Mrs. Morres, stated Mrs. Morres had told of her mother walking Mrs. Morres and a sister, when they were small children, from Bodie to the school, a distance of 115 miles. Mrs. Morres' mother did this to enroll the girls in the school.

Mrs. Morres recalled that her brother, Bob, attended the Indian school under different circumstances. School officials picked him up without notification and the family did not know what had happened to him for several days. She said this was not an uncommon occurrence in those early days—but the federal government was entrusted with the responsibility to see that Indian children were provided an education and they would "round them up" and enroll them in school without contacting the parents.

Mrs. Morres said her father worked in the mines of Bodie. When the winter weather turned bitter, the family would move to Hawthorne,

Nevada, remaining there until the following spring.[17]

Ross Morres, a son of Mrs. Morres, who resides in Fairfax, Virginia, also interviewed with his mother, explained Indians were not considered United States citizens until 1924, with the exception of those men who served in the armed forces during World war I. Prior to that time Indians were considered as "non-persons," he said. He further explained the operation of Indian schools, such as Stewart. The children would remain at the school, living in residence quarters under the supervision of the Bureau of Indian Affairs. Often the children, living at home, would just "disappear," as did Mrs. Morres' brother, and it might be months before the parents were informed their children were at the school. A number of Indian children from Bodie were enrolled in this fashion and obtained their education at Stewart.[18]

The first class to graduate from the Stewart school received diplomas in 1901. Class members represented the Paiute, Shoshone and Washoe tribes.

This story appeared on the front page of the April 20, 1911 issue of the Bridgeport Chronicle-Union and Bodie Chronicle, in the early 1900's, the Mono County seat newspaper in Bridgeport, California:

THUS WAS TRUE LOVE REWARDED

"A youngster in one of the Mono County schools, asked to write a composition under the title, 'TRUE LOVE REWARDED', offered the following:

"Once on a time there was a little girl and a little boy lived near each other and played together. They growed and went to school together and liked each other very much. When they was a man and a woman they loved each other dearly and was married and lived happy in a nice home he got. But one thing made them sad and that was because they didn't have no children. One day a great war broke out and the man went to fight for his country. He was gone away for six years and became a general, but he longed for the time when he could go home to his loving wife. At last the cruel war was ended and the man hurried home, and O, what was his joy when his wife presented him with four little children she had got while he was gone. Thus was true love rewarded."[19]

FOOTNOTES — CHAPTER 2

1. W.T. Elliott, Common Schools Report, 1877-1878

2. Everett O'Rourke, "The Highest School in California," page 10

3. Warren Loose, "Bodie Bonanza, The True Story of A Flamboyant Past," page 54

4. Bodie Standard, January 9, 1879

5. W.T. Elliott, Common Schools Report, 1878-1879

6. Mrs. C.W. Sullivan, Common Schools Report, 1879-1880

7. Cornelia Richards, 1900-1901 County Superintendent Report

8. Everett V. O'Rourke, "The Highest School in California," page 21

9. Emil W. Billeb, "Mining Camp Days," page 83

10. O'Rourke, "The Highest School in California," page 23

11. Kent Pierce, an interview

12. Voter Registration Records, Mono County

13. Bodie Evening Miner, August 12, 1881

14. Ibid, August 13, 1881

15. Ibid, August 2, 188

16. Ibid, August 8, 1881

17. Mrs. Anne W. Morres, an interview

18. Ross Morres, an interview

19. Bridgeport Chronicle-Union and Bodie Chronicle, April 20, 1911

CHAPTER 3

"THE BODIE 601"—VIGILANTES!

In the checkered history of Bodie crime, most of which occurred between 1878 and 1882, without doubt the most notorious event involved the murder of one Thomas Treloar by Joseph (Frenchy) DaRoche (also spelled DeRoche), and the subsequent lynching of DaRoche by a mob calling itself "Bodie 601."

Surprisingly, it was Bodie's one and only lynching.

Both deaths occurred at the exact same spot—in the center of town in front of the Miners Union Hall, a building that now houses the Bodie Museum. The lynch mob had decided that their victim must die for his crime where he had shot and killed his victim.

During the latter part of the 19th century, the term "601" was a popular title used throughout the West for a vigilance committee. In Virginia City, Nevada, lawlessness had reached a peak during 1871… "seemingly from nowhere there sprang into being a secret organization known as the Six Hundred and One, a masked group of vigilantes, whose rapid dispensation of fatal justice was accomplished in the dead of night without benefit of court and jury trial…. Near midnight on March 24, 1871, at least a few Comstock Citizens witnessed the 601 in action—the victim being Arthur Perkins Heffernan." A few years later, the "601" emerged in the old railroad town of Truckee, California in the years 1874 and 1875 when the townspeople there, fed up with lawlessness, established a vigilance group and named it "Truckee 601." Its purpose was to rid the community of lawless characters and it thrived until a member was mistakenly shot by a fellow member. The 601 disbanded, but reappeared in 1889, only to again disband in August of that year, never to be heard from again. "John Law" had taken over. A plaque, dedicated to "Truckee 601" can be seen today on Truckee's main street.

"Bad Man From Bodie" stories abound. The booming gold and silver mining community deserved every derogatory epithet attributed to it.

The January 14, 1881 murder of Treloar and DaRoche's subsequent lynching January 17, three days later, deserve special mention.

The "601" in Bodie acted as a lynch mob only once. Threats of "601" action often served to keep the peace, at least temporarily, and twice previously vigilance activities did occur—both times by groups of miners, one of which ended in the shooting death of a miner. Neither incident was by direct action of the committee as a whole, however. After its one and only lynching, the "Bodie 601" was never heard from again.

TRUCKEE "601": This monument stands on Truckee, California's main street as a reminder of the vigilante committee that carried out its own type of law enforcement in the 1870s. (A Doug Brodie photo)

When the Treloar incident began, the Bridgeport Chronicle-Union of January 15, 1881 (the Mono County seat newspaper) reported on the murder as follows:

"ANOTHER FOUL MURDER—Again Bodie comes to the front with another murder—the foulest of the many that have disgraced that town. Yesterday morning at half-past one o'clock, Joseph DaRoche, a French-Canadian, shot to death Thomas Treloar, a Cornish miner. It appears to have been a cold-blooded murder of a peaceable and harmless citizen by a notorious desperado, and, to add enormity to the crime, the custody of the murderer was entrusted to a drunken constable, being removed from the jail for that purpose, and consequently he escaped, Farnsworth, the constable, being oblivious to all except the prisoner offering him $1,000 to let him escape.

MINERS UNION HALL: This building was the site of most
of the town's social and political functions and was the scene of Bodie's one
and only lynching in the winter of 1881. (A Jim Watson photo)

"DaRoche had attended the A.O.U.W. Ball (held in the Miners
Union Hall) and danced with Mrs. Treloar, against the request of her
husband. About the close of the ball DaRoche left the hall and laid in
wait for his victim at the corner of Main and Lowe streets, where Treloar
was shot through the head. Intense excitement prevailed against
DaRoche and Farnsworth, but DaRoche was quickly captured."[1]

The Chronicle-Union of January 2, 1881, carried this editorial based
upon what happened: "MUST BE PUNISHED—After a score—more
or less—of murders committed in Bodie during the past two years, for
which not one of the murderers received his deserts—excepting a poor
devil of a Chinaman—DaRoche, the murderer of Treloar, was hanged by
Judge Lynch in that town at an early hour on Monday morning over the
spot where the murder was committed. It is to be regretted that the criminal history of this county caused the people of Bodie to administer justice themselves to the murderer, instead of allowing the law to take its
course and turn the murderer loose, but it must be admitted that the
members of the "Bodie 601" had the moral support of the community,
and it is hoped the lesson taught on the streets of Bodie on Sunday, and
Monday morning last, will be a salutary one to the rougher element of
that town. No county in the State can boast of more honorable judges
and efficient sheriffs than Mono, and if the members of the legal profes-

sion, of which we have many of the ablest, will but see that their clients have a speedy, fair and impartial trial, and not do their utmost to delay such important trials until witnesses spirit themselves away, there will be no necessity for Judge Lynch to open his court—but murderers must be punished."[2]

Perhaps DaRoche had reason to end the life of Thomas Treloar. In research by the authors, it was found that Treloar on at least one occasion had been arrested for beating Mrs. Treloar. A story in the Daily Bodie Standard of Monday, June 30, 1879, stated: for assaulting his wife, T.H. Treloar stood trial and was convicted.

If DaRoche had had a previous romantic interest in Mrs. Treloar, the fact that her husband had assaulted her on at least that one known occasion might be motive for the French Canadian's fatal shooting of Treloar. At the time of his lynching, when asked if he had any final statement, DaRoche said he had none.

The Coroner's Jury spent two days investigating the murder, including the questioning of two eyewitnesses, G.W. Alexander and E.S. Butler, who testified that they observed DaRoche shoot Treloar without provocation. The Jury found that the killing was "a willful and premeditated murder by DaRoche;" that Constable John Kirgan was "guilty of gross neglect of duty in allowing the prisoner to be removed from jail," and that Deputy Sheriff Joe Farnsworth was "criminally careless in allowing the escape of the prisoner."[3]

The editorial comment was followed by the Chronicle-Union's story of the events involving the actions of "Judge Lynch" with this story: "BODIE 601—DaRoche, the murderer of Treloar, was captured Saturday night, eight miles from Bodie, on the Goat Ranch Road, and hanged by the '601' on Monday morning. We clip the following account of the lynching from the (Bodie) Free Press:"

The Free Press story:

"Judge Lynch held his first court session in Bodie early on Monday morning and passed judgment on a criminal whose crime is already recorded and impressed upon every mind in this community. The tragic end of Joseph DaRoche, the murderer, was at once awful and impressive. The lesson to be learned from it is easily read and the simplest mind can fully comprehend it. That a cruel murder had been committed no one can deny; that the swift retribution was expected every observing citizen could predict with safety.

"The excitement of the Sabbath did not die away and the wrath of the people did not go out with the setting of the sun. As the shades of darkness enveloped the town, the spirit of revenge increased in intensity and developed into a blazing column of fire. It was burning in its intensity and fearful in its results. After the adjournment of the court and DaRoche was taken back to his narrow cell, a mysterious committee was organized, the like of which has existed in many towns on this coast since '46 and whose work has been quick and thorough. This committee, it is reported, held a long session and discussed the matter in hand. The session was long and deliberate, and its conclusions resulted in the lynching of DaRoche.

"Between 1:30 and 2 o'clock Monday morning a long line of masked and unmasked men were seen to file out of a side street into Bonanza Avenue. There must have been two hundred of them and as the march progressed to the jail the column increased. In front were the shotguns carried by determined men. They were backed up by a company which evidently meant business, and no ordinary force could foil them in their progress. When the jail was reached it was surrounded and the leader made a loud knock at the door. All was dark and quiet within. The cell had the effect of producing a dim light in the office, and amid loud cries of 'DaRoche,' 'Bring him out,' 'Open the door,' 'Hurry up,' etc., Jailer Kirgan appeared, and responded by saying: 'All right boys; wait a minute; give me a little time.'

"In a moment the outside door was opened slowly and four or five men entered. Under instructions the door of the cell in which the condemned prisoner lay was swung open. The poor wretch knew what this untimely visit meant, and prepared for the trying ordeal and humiliating death. It was some moments before he was brought out, and the crowd began to grow impatient. Some imagined the prisoner had been taken away by the officers. If this had been the case what would have followed can only be imagined. All these doubts were put to rest by the presence of the man. He wore light-colored pants, a colored calico shirt, and over his shoulders was hung a canvas coat buttoned around the neck. His head was bare, and as the bright rays of the moon glanced upon his face there was a picture of horror visible. It was a look of dogged and defiant submission. With a firm step he descended the steps and came out in a hurried manner, closely guarded by shotguns and revolvers. The order to fall in was given, and all persons not members of the mysterious committee to stand back. The march up Bonanza Street was rapid. Not a word was said by the condemned man, and his gaze was fixed upon the ground. He turned, and, when Webber's Blacksmith Shop was reached a belt was made.

"In front of this place was a huge gallows frame, used for raising up wagons, etc., while being repaired. Now it was to be used for a different purpose. 'Move it to the spot where the murder was committed,' was the order, and immediately it was picked up by a dozen men and was carried to the corner of Main and Lowe streets. The condemned man glanced at it for a moment and an apparent shudder came over him, but he uttered not a word. From an eye witness we learned that the scene which followed was awful in its impressiveness. The snow had just begun to fall, and the moon, which had shone so brightly during the early part of the night, shed but a pale light on the assembled company. When a corner was reached the heavy gallows was placed upon the ground and the prisoner led under it. The prisoner's demeanor still remained passive, and his hands, encased in irons, were clasped. His eyes occasionally were turned upward and his lips were seen to move once or twice. On each end of the frame were windlasses and large ropes attached. The rope placed around the prisoner's neck was a small one, when the knot was made it rested against the left ear. This did not suit DaRoche particularly and he changed it so that it was more in the rear. Some one suggested that his hands and legs should be tied. This was immediately done. The large iron hooks of the frame dangled near the prisoner and the grating sound produced a peculiar feeling. It was at least three minutes before everything was all ready.

"DaRoche was asked by the leader if he had anything to say. He replied: 'No; nothing.' In a moment he was again asked the same question and a French-speaking bystander was requested to receive his answer. The reply this time was: 'I have nothing to say only O God.' 'Pull him,' was the order and in a twinkling the body rose three feet from the ground. Previous to putting on the rope, the overcoat was removed. A second after the body was elevated a sudden twitch of the legs was observed, but with that exception, not a muscle moved while the body hung on the crossbeam. His death took place without a particle of pain. The face was placid, and the eyes closed and never were reopened. Strangulation must have been immediate. While the body swung to and fro, like pendulum of a clock, the crowd remained perfectly quiet.

"After a lapse of two or three minutes a voice, sharp and clear, was heard in the background: 'I will give $100 if twenty men connected with this affair will publish their names in the paper to-morrow morning.' The voice was immediately recognized as that of a leading attorney (reports were it was Patrick Reddy, Bodie's famous one-armed barrister), and a yell went up from the crowd. 'Give him the rope,' 'Put him out,' and similar sentences drowned out the man and his voice. His retreat was dignified as the exigencies of the case would admit of.

"While the body was still hanging a paper was pinned onto his breast bearing the following inscription: 'All others take warning. Let no one cut him down. Bodie 601.'

"At the expiration of thirty minutes Dr. Deal was summoned, and he pronounced life extinct. The body was then cut down, placed in a plain box and taken to Ward's undertaking rooms. The mysterious committee had completed its work, and the captain gave out the order 'All members of the Bodie 601 will meet at their rendezvous.' In a moment the scene of death was deserted. To use a familiar expression DaRoche died game. He was as firm as a rock to the last and passed out into the unknown without a shudder."[4]

Undoubtedly this graphic description of the work of the "Bodie 601" was repeated and reprinted widely and had a decided affect on those law-breakers who might have practiced their wares in Bodie. They probably thought twice before carrying out their black art. Although more crime was to follow, the 601 never called upon "Judge Lynch" to assist them.

An indication of the downtrend in Bodie in 1881 was this news story: CHANGING—Hotels, restaurants and saloons in Bodie are as change-able as the stock market. Bodie House, W. A. Johnson, Occidental, Kemp and Colman, Mono, King & Bennett, Noonday, Josiah Brown had not changed. Barney Clark, William Davison, Pat Fahey, A.A. Carion, Cullan & McDermott and Alex Whitman's saloons—six of over 100, have not changed (indicating all the others had). In almost every instance, the changes had resulted disastrously to creditors.[5]

But crime took no holiday and the Bridgeport Chronicle-Union of April 2 that year reported: "MORE SHOOTING—After a short respite, Bodie again looms into notoriety by shots from the revolver. This time it is a fracas between two disreputable men in a house on the noted Bonanza Street. Both were shot—one dangerously. Price, the assailant, was arrested."[6]

The same newspaper: "JUSTIFIABLE HOMICIDE—On Saturday night last, at Bodie, Officer John Roberts shot to death John Myers, a noted and disreputable character of that town, one who threatened to kill Roberts on sight. Justice Phlegar discharged Roberts holding that it was justifiable—and so say all good citizens.[7] And a story in the Bridgeport paper just 10 days later, June 14: "AND YET ANOTHER—Here comes another, and of course, it's from Bodie. On Tuesday morning last, 'breakfast' time, David T. Hitchell was shot to death in an opium den. James Stockdale was arrested and examined for the murder, and discharged. The people were satisfied to lose such, and don't care to throw away three or four thousand dollars in trying to find who shot him. [8]

Perhaps we should call this "Justice at any cost."

BODIE'S JAIL TODAY: In its checkered past, this structure held most of
the town's famous and infamous outlaws and cutthroats, including the
community's only lynching victim, Joseph (Frenchy) DaRoche.
(A Jim Watson photo)

Just four days later, June 18, the Chronicle-Union carried this story: "MURDER TRIALS—For the first time in the history of this (Mono) county for the past two years our county jail does not contain a single murderer, the last one, Sam Chung, having walked out a free man, he having been pronounced 'not guilty' by a jury of taxpayers of this county.

"That the people of this county believe Sam Chung to be guilty of murder of the Mexican is not to be denied, but the prosecution failed at every trial to obtain a conviction, but on this third trial it secured an acquittal—a verdict that meets with the approval of the taxpayers of the county when the weakness of the prosecution is taken in consideration."[9] From the sound of the story, the newspaper had Sam Chung convicted, regardless of the jury's decision.

The Chronicle-Union of Aug. 13: "INDIAN MURDER—The Bridgeport Indians tell us that an Indian murdered his squaw in Bodie a few days ago by splitting her head. The wide-awake local of the Free Press hasn't dropped on it if such a murder occurred. Probably the Indians have kept mum about the subject."[10]

Following the DaRoche lynching an opposition organization called The Law And Order League was formed. Its influence was limited and the shooting of several of its members following a meeting led to its demise within a few months. It is assumed, however, that as a result of actions by the "601" and the Law and Order League, some lawbreakers on occasion did go to prison and pay for their crimes, although the percentage was minimal.

Ironically, never mentioned in the press at the time of the DaRoche lynching, was the absence of law enforcement. Bodie had local elected constables on duty, and, since it was not incorporated, the Mono County Sheriff's Office patrolled the town with deputies. None seemed to be available to save DaRoche, and the deputy sheriff-jailer, John F. Kirgan, was of little help against the angry members of the "601." It appeared that when thugs and "bad men" killed their own kind, or when a shooting occurred in an opium den, the citizenry remained more or less unconcerned, but when violence involved a well-known citizen or involved the mining unions and the companies, then the town became upset, and in the case of the Treloar-DaRoche incident, became so outraged it took matters into its own hands.

Mentioned in the DaRoche lynching news article was the jailer on duty when DaRoche escaped, a "Farnsworth" identified as "a drunken constable" by the Bridgeport Chronicle-Union, which stated he had accepted $1,000 from DaRoche for allowing DaRoche to escape. Farnsworth had been on night duty and apparently took a few too many drinks while visiting various Bodie bars.

Mono County Sheriff's deputy and Bodie Jailer Joe Farnsworth had taken DaRoche to his room at the Standard Boarding House for safe keeping with the approval of the Constable, and also a sheriff's deputy John Kirgan, (the same man who was on duty later when the 601 did show up) after it was learned a lynch mob might storm the jail. Farnsworth stated he had tied DaRoche to the bed and then fell asleep. When he failed to show up at the jail the following morning, Kirgan went to Farnsworth's room to find Farnsworth asleep and DaRoche missing. When Kirgan indicated that Farnsworth might be involved in a conspiracy to allow DaRoche to escape, Farnsworth denied it, but did admit DaRoche had offered him a $1,000 bribe. Bodie citizens by now were outraged by the murder, the subsequent escape of the alleged perpetrator, and by the fact Farnsworth allowed the escape. Groups of searchers were not only trying to recapture DaRoche, but they were after Farnsworth who, they declared, "Must produce the murderer or take the consequences," according to the Free Press.

Farnsworth left town to escape the wrath of the crowd. From Carson City he wrote the Bodie Free Press to deny taking money from DaRoche and challenge anyone to prove that he had. After several months he returned to Bodie only to find he had lost his job as a sheriff's deputy. Kirgan, too, was later removed as Bodie jailer by the Mono County Sheriff. He did remain as constable, a position to which he had been elected.

An example of vigilante activity elsewhere appeared in the Bodie Evening Miner issue of May 23, 1882: "VIGILANTES IN MONTANA (Special to the Evening Miner), Butte City: A circular has been issued here, signed '3777' which reads as follows: 'To burglars, thieves, bummers, tramps and all able-bodied men and boys soliciting aid from door to door—you are hereby ordered to leave this city and vicinity without further notice or take the consequences. Families throughout the city and vicinity are requested to refuse alms to any able-bodied tramp who may apply to them for the same.' The circular is issued by a vigilance committee who mean business."[11]

The derivation of the vigilante term "601" is believed to be a comment at an early-day lynching when someone shouted, "Six Feet Under / No Trial / One Rope!" hence, "Six-O-One."

FOOTNOTES — CHAPTER 3

1. Bridgeport Chronicle-Union, January 15, 1881
2. Ibid, January 2, 1881
3. Bodie Daily Free Press, January 16, 1881
4. Bridgeport Chronicle-Union, February 3, 1881
5. Ibid, March 5, 1881
6. Ibid, April 2, 1881
7. Ibid, June 2, 1881
8. Ibid, June 14, 1881
9. Ibid, June 18, 1881
10. Ibid, August 13, 1881
11. Bodie Evening Miner, April 2, 1881

CHAPTER 4

ANNA ALENA DECHAMBEAU MCKENZIE

This is the story of Anna Alena DeChambeau McKenzie.

She was born May 8, 1896 on the DeChambeau family ranch at Mono Lake in a dwelling that still stands. She married Mervin J. McKenzie in the Township of Bodie at the age of 21. Her husband's nicknames were "Merve" and "Mac" and his family for many years owned the McKenzie Brewery in Bodie.

These recollections were passed on to one of the authors, James Watson, by Mrs. McKenzie in 1989. She has since passed away.[1]

Annie's father, uncle and grandfather arrived in Bodie in 1880 and sent to Canada for her grandmother soon thereafter. Her grandmother, Marian Alena DeChambeau, remained in Bodie until 1917, when she was in her 70's. She then moved to the family ranch at Mono Lake. She died about 1920. Annie's grandfather then left Mono Lake, lived for a short time in a cabin near Silver Lake, making a living, catching and selling fish to area residents. He became ill, moved to Idaho, and communications with the family ceased.

Annie's father, Louis DeChambeau, owned the Mono Lake ranch and worked at the lumber mill in Lundy as a millwright. He would ride his horse to work during the summer months and ski to work in the winter. Louis worked on the ranch when not employed in Lundy. He developed his carpentry skills and made sleighs for sale and developed a skill for manufacturing skis. He proved to be an excellent skier and was rated second only to Snow Shoe Thompson, a legendary skier—one of the first in the West—who many times skied over the Sierra Nevada Mountains to Genoa, Nevada, carrying the U.S. Mail. Skis, when first manufactured, were referred to as 'snow shoes', hence the nickname, Snow Shoe Thompson, and doubtless he was the first to ride a pair of skis from Tioga to Lundy. He made skis for sale, and at first he sold them for five dollars a pair and a dollar for a pole...men's skis were nine feet long, and women's were seven.[2]

DeChambeau's grandson, the late Kent DeChambeau of Sacramento, told the authors his grandfather, at one time manufactured a special pair of skis for Snow Shoe Thompson.

Annie spent many summer vacations at Grandmother DeChambeau's Boarding House, which stands today next door to the IOOF Hall on Bodie's Main Street, sometimes referred to as the DeChambeau Hotel. She recalled that the boarding house shared the entry stairs—Grandma's entry was on the second floor left, and on the right was the entry to the Odd Fellows Hall where the Rebekah Lodge met as well as the Oddfellows. The "hall" side of the building contained recreational facilities—ping pong, bowling, etc.

Annie recalled that the first floor of Grandma's boarding house had three apartments, and these were rented to men with families. The building caretaker, Dave Smith, whom she referred to as "The Bachelor," made his quarters at the rear of the first floor, and a sink with a pump was located there. The second floor contained 12 small rooms in dormitory style. These, she recalls, were rented to single miners.

DeCHAMBEAU BOARDING HOUSE: Annie's Grandmother
DeChambeau is photographed in front of her boarding house, a brick
structure that still stands next to the Odd Fellows Hall. Beside her is the
caretaker, Dave Smith, whom she referred to as "The Bachelor."
(By permission of Kent DeChambeau)

Her grandmother had six men in the upstairs bedrooms plus her own apartment and two apartments downstairs in the back part of the structure. Smith was a carpenter and cabinetmaker and had his shop in the area in which his living quarters were located. Her uncle Jack, and a brother, Herb DeChambeau, helped her grandmother with her horse and buggy which were quartered in a stable at the rear of the boarding house. Since the stoves used wood for fuel, they also helped out by carrying wood up the back stairs. It would be stored in a vacant room she kept for that purpose. Grandma's living quarters were located at the rear of the second floor.

Annie recalled that the building served as a rooming house for the entire time her grandmother occupied it—until 1917. At that time it was taken over by Bodie Mike (Mike Lazovitch) until 1920. Bodie Mike opened a bar on the ground floor. Annie recalled that this upset the DeChambeau family. Lazovitch later moved his saloon to Lee Vining. It is called "Bodie Mike's."

When Annie's father arrived in Bodie he hauled and sold firewood for a living, cutting the wood near Table Mountain in the Hawthorne area. She recalled that her father fashioned a tool similar to a pair of pliers. These, she said, were used to cut the shackles from the body of a man who had met his maker by being hanged. Her father had made the tool at the blacksmith shop located behind Grandma DeChambeau's Rooming House.

The man Annie referred to must have been Joseph "Frenchy" DaRoche, who was lynched January 17, 1881, by the "Bodie 601" at the corner of Main and Lowe streets following the January 14 murder of Thomas Treloar, a Bodie miner. DaRoche was shackled hand and foot by the mob, and was left swinging at the end of a noose, with his hands and feet still bound. He was cut down 30 minutes later, pronounced dead by Dr. Deal, and taken to Ward's Mortuary.[3] It probably was at the mortuary that Anna's father was asked to cut the shackles. No other hangings are reported in Bodie historical writings, and the State of California carried out most of its death penalty hangings at Folsom Prison. A few were conducted elsewhere in the state, but not in Bodie.

Annie recalled she and "Mac" were married in 1917. Mac arrived by horse and sled at the ranch at Mono Lake, picked up Annie, and together they traveled to Bodie by sled through the snow where they tied the marital knot. The McKenzie family had closed their brewery prior to 1917 and moved to San Francisco. Mac remained in Bodie.

TURN-OF-THE-CENTURY BODIE: Still a community with many buildings, the Standard Mill is in the foreground. Main Street has many businesses and at the left near the end of a line of structures facing east are the DeChambeau Hotel the Odd Fellows Hall, an open lot, and then the Miners Union Hall, now the park museum. The 1932 fire destroyed many of the other buildings. (By permission of Eastern California Museum)

The brewery had consisted of a saloon in front, a residence in the center and the brewery in the rear. Annie and Mac moved into the residence and their first child, a daughter, was born there. Because Bodie's population had dwindled, the attending physician had to travel to Bodie from Aurora, about 16 miles by rough road. Annie also was attended by a midwife, or, as Annie preferred to call her, a practical nurse, named Annie Fuller. Annie Fuller was an Andrews, she married Mr. Fuller, and "took care of all the babies in Bodie," Annie recalled.

Mac was employed by J. S. Cain hauling old iron from a mill in Bodie by truck to Hawthorne. The iron was transferred to rail cars there and shipped to San Francisco for scrap. Mac also drove the stagecoach mail route from Bodie to Del Monte, working for Cecil Berkum. She explained Del Monte was midway between Bodie and Aurora, about 6 miles. A truck would travel from Hawthorne with mail and supplies and would meet the stages from Bodie and Aurora. The stages would change to fresh horses and return to Bodie and Aurora with the mail and supplies.

The trip was made daily. In the winter "snowshoes" would be attached to the horses' hooves, enabling them to pull the stage sleds. Annie recalled the snowshoes appeared to be pieces of rubber cut from conveyor belts from the mill. She also referred to them as "skis."

Mac and Annie made their home in the abandoned brewery from 1917 through 1920 and after their daughter was born they occupied a dwelling near the school on Green Street. Annie said the house was owned by Pearl Matley. Following a short stay there they moved to a house on the hill near the mill and near the Boone family. Their next move was to the power house at Green Creek (the historic hydroelectric plant that generated the first power in the history of the world to be transported by wire (square) to another source—Bodie—for use). This was shortly after 1920 and Mac worked there as plant operator for J.S. Cain, the owner. She stated there were two houses at Green Creek and she and Mac occupied one and Jimmie Cain, eldest son of J.S. Cain, lived in the other. Mac and Jimmie each worked 12-hour shifts seven days a week. After a year Jimmie left his job and Annie's cousin, Willie Miller of Bodie, took his job. Annie and Mac moved from Green Creek in 1924 to Mono Lake and then to Mill Creek.

Annie recalled the March 7, 1911 avalanche of snow that wiped out the nearby hydroelectric plant at Copper Mountain which killed seven persons.

Annie and Mac eventually moved from Mill Creek to Oakland where Mac entered the meat business with a brother. They returned to Mill Creek after two years and Mac went to work again for J.S. Cain's Pacific Power Company. The couple then moved to Manhattan, Nevada; Silver Lake, Rush Creek, June Lake, and from 1930 to 1961 to the Pacific Power Company control station where Mac retired. He died in 1967 in Bishop.

Annie recalled a Bodie character named Billy LaGross, also refered to as Billy Gross, and by early Bodie residents as "Buffalo Billy." She stated he lived in a cabin near Chinatown. Billy had curly hair and rode an old horse. He did some traveling and Annie remembered him as often riding through her father's ranch at Mono Lake on his way back to Bodie. He was known, she said, as having "sticky fingers" and would make his living "picking up things" that didn't belong to him, and selling them. Her last recollection of Billy was his cabin exploding and burning to the ground.

"Buffalo Billy was attempting to dry some firewood in the cook stove," Annie said. "He told people later he had stored dynamite in his woodpile and had grabbed some of it by mistake, but many thought his sticky fingers were busy in someone else's woodpile, the owner of which is thought to have laced some of the wood 'borrowed' by Billy with dynamite. Hence, the mighty blast," Annie concluded with a laugh. (Although Annie is gone now, we thank her for sharing her recollections. (D&J).

FOOTNOTES — CHAPTER 4

1. An interview with Mrs. Anna McKenzie
2. Joseph N. LeConte, "A Summer Of Travel in the HIGH SIERRA," pages 50, 51
3. Bridgeport Chronicle-Union, January 22, 1881

CHAPTER 5

A TRIP TO MONO LAKE

Mono Lake, referred to by some as "The Dead Sea of the West," has played a fascinating part in the history of Bodie. Located 15 miles south of the mining town, it was circumvented in 1881 at its eastern edge by a railroad that extended from Mono Mills at the south to Bodie.

Boats plied the lake, transporting material to build the railroad and to haul wood products and lumber. References to the lake were made during the 19th Century by geologists, authors, explorers and prospectors in writings about the Eastern Sierra Nevada Mountains. Some provide an idea about how the high Sierra pioneers lived in the Bodie area during the 1860s, 1870s, and 1880s. Any trip to Bodie is incomplete without a visit to Mono Lake.

Mark Twain (Samuel Clemens) was a visitor to the area in the 1860s, and he wrote about his experiences. His descriptive prose describing Mono Lake was included later in his book, "Roughing It." Before concentrating on Twain's writings it is interesting to observe the area through the eyes and words of other writers and explorers.

Israel C. Russell, a geologist, prepared a descriptive report of the Mono Lake basin and surrounding environs in 1883, which was printed with the unlikely title of "Quaternary History of Mono Valley, California." The word, quaternary, as applied by Russell means; "of, relating to, or being the geological period from the end of the tertiary period (in this instance the formation of high mountains) to the present time or the corresponding system of rocks," meaning the time in history in which the area was formed.

As a geologist of the day, Russell visited the Mono Valley three times, first in 1880, the period in which Bodie, just a few miles north of Mono Lake, was in its heyday. He returned to the area later in 1881, but was forced to leave due to winter weather. He returned in 1882 to complete his study and his lucid prose helps greatly in understanding the development of Bodie and environs, although he never saw the town.

Russell wrote: "The most practicable route for reaching Lake Mono from the east is by rail to Reno, Nevada, thence by the Carson and Colorado Railroad to the town of Hawthorne, situated at the end of Walker Lake, and thence by a well-constructed mountain road which winds and zigzags up the steep eastern slope of the Walker River or Wassuc Mountains, at the foot of which Hawthorne is situated. This road is a monument to Western enterprise, and owes its construction mainly to the development of the rich silver mines of Bodie. (Russell's reference was partially correct: Bodie actually was noted more for its gold mines than for silver; Aurora more for silver than for gold).

"At present there is no railroad connection with Mono Valley; we therefore make the journey from Hawthorne to Aurora by stage… explorers in the far West have found that the most practicable method of carrying forward their work is to travel on mule back, the desert character of much of the country and the consequent scarcity of grass and water making the use of horses less satisfactory. From Aurora, therefore, as there are no public conveyances leading through the section we wish to examine, we will continue our journey in the saddle.

"We pass on down the sloping plain leading to Lake Mono, and after a monotonous ride of ten or twelve miles through sage-brush, over sand dunes, and across ancient lake beaches, reach Warm Springs, on the eastern shore of the lake. When I gained this camping place in the spring of 1881, the only evidence that it had been frequented by man was a trail leading to a spring. A year later I found a railroad crossing the valley, and a station near where I had previously camped. This is the Bodie and Benton Railroad, at present incomplete, which connects Bodie with the pine forests clothing portions of the eastern border of Mono Valley."[1]

The Bodie Railway & Lumber Company rail line began operations between Bodie and Mono Mills in November, 1881, with a station at Warm Springs. It proved so successful plans called for an extension from Warm Springs east to Benton where it would connect with the Carson & Colorado Railroad and eventually provide a rail connection to the outside world. The name, therefore, was changed to Bodie & Benton Railroad and work on the extension began. Russell may have observed this extension, nine miles of which was graded when the project was halted and never completed.

TUFA AT MONO LAKE: Spires such as these are located in and around
Mono Lake, just south of Bodie, at the edge of the town of Lee Vining.
They are created as springs beneath the lake add water and bring forth
alkaline which forms the spires. The tufa thus exposed originally was under
water. Much still is. (A Jim Watson photo)

Russell tells, too, of strange phenomena involving Mono Lake. He writes: "Strolling along the shore we find windrows thrown up by the waves, not only of sand and gravel... but also of the larval cases of a fly that inhabits the lake in countless myriads. These larvae are used by the Piute Indians for food. During the autumn, Indian encampments may be found all about the lake; while women, in picturesque groups, may be seen gathering the food as it is thrown ashore by the waves. The partially dried larvae, the kernels, are separated from the enclosing cases, the chaff, by winnowing in the wind with the aid of a scoop-shaped basket; they are then tossed into large conical baskets, which the women carry on their backs."

Russell again describes this phenomena while telling of still another peculiarity of Mono Lake, but describing first problems due to the lack of irrigation water:

"At a distance of a few miles we pass a rude cabin near the lake shore, where Louis Sammon, the pioneer of the valley, has made his home. There are a few other humble habitations on the southern and western borders of the lake, some of which are surrounded by meadowlands and grain fields of small extent; but nearly the entire valley is without the limit of cultivation for the reason that water can not be had for irrigation. There was formerly sufficient wild grass in many portions of the basin to support considerable numbers of cattle and sheep; but, owing to over-stocking, these natural pastures are now nearly ruined.

"If the day chance to be stormy, we shall see an effect of the wind on the waters that but few lakes present. Lake Mono, as already stated, is strongly charged with alkaline salts; when it is agitated by the wind, the waves break into foam which gathers along the leeward shore in a band many rods wide and sometimes several feet thick. Sheets of this tenacious froth are caught up in the wind and driven inland through the desert shrubs in fluffy masses that look like balls of cotton. This peculiar effect of strong winds on alkaline waters is highly picturesque and adds greatly to the beauty of the lake.

"Owing to the chemical character of its waters, Lake Mono is unin-habited by fishes or mollusks, but it swarms with countless myriads of small crustaceans, known as brine shrimps, and the larvae of a fly, as mentioned before, are seen about its borders in immense swarms during certain seasons. In autumn and early winter the lake surface is literally darkened with countless numbers of ducks, swans, gulls, grebes, and other aquatic birds, attracted thither by the brine shrimps and larvae."

Unfortunately the composition of land and water and man's interac-tion with nature is such that the Mono Lake of today is unlike the Mono Lake of the 1880s. No froth is blown up by the winds these days and the many wild birds that were so profuse have dwindled, but there is much hope for improvement.

Russell describes his selection of the names for the two islands in Mono Lake:

"While riding along the shore of Mono Lake, one's attention is con-tinually attracted to the islands that break the monotony of its surface. The largest of these is remarkable for its light gray color, which makes it appear almost white in comparison with the second in size, which is near-ly black. In proceeding with our studies, we shall see that the color of these islands is of geological significance. In seeking for names by which to designate them, it was suggested that their differences in color might be used, but the writer preferred to record some of the poetic words from the language of the Aboriginal inhabitants of the valley. On the larger island there are hot springs and orifices through which heated vapors escape, which are among the most interesting features of the basin. In the legends of the Pa-vi-o-si people, who still inhabit the region in scattered bands, there is a story about diminutive spirits, having long wavy hair, that are sometimes seen in the vapor wreaths ascending from hot springs. The word 'Pa-o-ha' (a footnote here states the aboriginal words, used in this paper for the first time as proper names, are from manuscript notes on the Indian Languages of the West by J. W. Powell) by which these spirits are known, is also used at times to designate hot springs in general.

"We may therefore name the large island 'Paoha Island', in remembrance, perhaps of the children of the mist that held their revels there on moonlit nights in times long past.

"The island second in size we call 'Negit Island,' the name being 'Pa-vi-o-osi, the word for blue-winged goose'."

Research indicates no such bird as a blue-winged goose exists and it is presumed the Pa-vi-o-osi were referring to our modern day seagull. Many of these birds exist inland, hundreds of miles from the ocean.

Additional research of the Mono Lake phenomena by the authors revealed an article in the Bodie Standard News of August 23, 1880, that mentioned the Mono Lake larvae referred to by Russell: "About 1,500 Piutes are gathered at the northeast corner of Mono Lake holding their annual festival. This consists of feasting, drinking, horse racing and going through the war dance. It is a sort of love feast where the dusky sons of the forest meet to select their mates. The grand war dance of the season comes off this evening, after which it will taper off by degrees, as each of the tribe lays in his stock of 'grub' from the lake, until the camp is deserted." Warren Loose referred in his book to the larval swarms: "This annual food harvesting event on the shore of Mono Lake by the Piutes had been a big event for hundreds of years in the life cycle of countless generations of these Indians. The grub, unpalatable to the finicky white man, was the larvae of a small fly in the form of a white worm which is thrown, in immense quantities, upon the shores of the lake. These larvae, when dried, were used by the Indians... as an important article of food. This grub the Piutes dubbed 'koo-cha-bee'."[2]

A prediction in 1883 by Russell is included in his report: "Should labor and transportation become cheaper in the Far West or should the demand for sodium carbonate increase, the waters of Lake Mono will afford the basis for an extensive industry. The desert tracts bordering the lake on the north offer advantageous sites for solar evaporation, while the forests of the Sierra will afford fuel for artificial evaporation should this be found more economical."[3]

Russell was predicting the harvesting of salt from the waters of Mono Lake for use in soaps and chemicals. This did not occur.

As part of his survey Russell also named two other Mono Lake landmarks which carry these designations to this day. The first was "Panum Crater," one of the 20 distinguishable craters in the lake vicinity, and which he terms a double crater, in which rough crags are piled in the center of the bowl—ejections of molten rock. The other is the "Aeolian Buttes," which Russell describes as fine examples of wind erosion. They are two small buttes near the Mono Craters and are composed of pink rhyolite.

Another description of the lake's phenomena comes from the pen of J. Ross Browne, artist, author and correspondent in the 1860s for Harper's New Monthly Magazine, a popular periodical of the day. Coincidently, Browne visited Aurora, Bodie, and what he termed "The Dead Sea of the West (Mono Lake)" in 1863, twenty years before Russell. Browne wrote at that time:

"A curious and rather disgusting deposit of worms about two feet high by three or four in thickness, extends like a vast rim around the shores of the lake. I saw no end to it during a walk of several miles along the beach. These worms are the larvae of flies, originally deposited in a floating tissue on the surface of the water. So far as I could discover most of them were dead. They lay in a solid oily mass, exhaling a peculiar though not unpleasant odor in the sun. Swarms of small black flies covered them to a depth of several inches.

"Such was the multitude of these flies that my progress was frequently arrested by them as they flew up. Whether they were engaged in an attempt to identify their own progeny, or, cannibal-like, were devouring the children of their enemies, it was impossible to determine. The former seemed to be rather a hopeless undertaking amid such a mixed crowd. The air for a circle of several yards was blackened with these flies, and their buzz sounded like the brewing of a distant storm. My eyes, nose, mouth, and ears were filled. I could not beat them off. Wherever they lit there they remained, sluggish and slimy. I fain had to rush out of the reach and seek a breathing-place some distance from the festive scene.

"It would appear that the worms, as soon as they attain the power of locomotion, creep up from the water, or are deposited on the beach by the waves during some of those violent gales which prevail in this region. The Mono Indians derive from them a fruitful source of subsistence. By drying them in the sun and mixing them with acorns, berries, grass-seeds, and other articles of food gathered up in the mountains, they make a conglomerate called 'cuchaba,' which they use as a kind of bread. I am told it is very nutritious and not at all unpalatable. The worms are also eaten in their natural condition. It is considered a delicacy to fry them in their own grease. When properly prepared by a skillful cook they resemble pork 'cracklings'.

"I was not hungry enough to require one of these dishes during my sojourn, but would recommend any friend who may visit the lake to eat a pound or two and let me know the result at his earliest convenience. In fact, I don't yearn for fat worms as an article of diet, though almost any kind of food is acceptable when my appetite is good. There must be hundreds perhaps thousands of thousands of tons of these oleaginous insects cast up on the beach every year. There is no danger of starvation on the shores of Mono. The inhabitants may be snowed in, flooded out, or cut off by Aboriginal hordes, but they can always rely upon the beach for fat meat. No other insect or animal that I could hear of exists in the waters of the lake."[4]

And now return to Mark Twain and his descriptive words of Mono Lake from "Roughing It." Twain visited the area at almost the same time as did Browne, although his book and descriptions did not reach publication until early in 1872.

Mono Lake, he writes, "is a lifeless, treeless, hideous desert, eight thousand feet above the level of the sea, and is guarded by mountains two thousand feet higher, whose summits are always clothed in clouds. This solemn, silent, sailless sea—this lonely tenant of the loneliest spot on earth—is little graced with the picturesque. It is an unpretending expanse of grayish water, about a hundred miles in circumference, with two islands in its centre..."

Twain describes the high alkali content of the water... "There are no fish in Mono Lake—no frogs, no snakes, no polliwogs—nothing, in fact, that goes to make life desirable. Millions of wild ducks and sea-gulls swim about the surface, but no living thing exists under the surface, except a white feathery sort of worm, one half an inch long, which looks like a bit of white thread frayed out at the sides. If you dip up a gallon of water, you will get about fifteen thousand of these. They give to the water a sort of grayish-white appearance. Then there is a fly, which looks something like our house fly. These settle on the beach to eat the worms that wash ashore—and at any time, you can see there a belt of flies an inch deep and six feet wide, and this belt extends clear around the lake—a belt of flies one hundred miles long. If you throw a stone among them, they swarm up so thick that they look dense, like a cloud. You can hold them under water as long as you please—they do not mind it. When you let them go, they pop up to the surface as dry as a patent office report, and walk off as unconcernedly as if they had been educated especially with a view to affording instructive entertainment to man in that particular way. Providence leaves nothing to go by chance."[5]

Modern-day Mono Lake in some ways resembles Mark Twain's descriptive words, but the lake certainly has had its problems since the visits by Russell, Browne and Twain. Around the turn of the Twentieth Century the City of Los Angeles lay claim to much of the water that fed Mono Lake and until the mid-1980s took this water. Court decisions began piling up against the city's eastern Sierra water rights when finally a 17-year campaign to save the alkaline, fishless lake was won and much of the water was again allowed to flow into the rapidly-depleting waterway which had begun shrinking when its tributaries began to dry up. The shrinkage stranded the eerie tufa towers of limestone formed from freshwater springs flowing from the lake bottom. The shrinkage not only stranded the towers but also posed a mortal threat to a major refuge for birds and the unique brine flies and brine shrimp described by those early visitors.

With the 1994-95 winter's phenomenally heavy snow, the lake rose four feet and precipitation in following winters has largely restored natural stream flow. It should push the level up another thirteen feet over the next two to four decades, say the experts. The stream restoration is "monumental," according to Scott Stine, a geomorphologist at California State University, Hayward. Until the lake rises that additional thirteen feet, the City of Los Angeles will be allowed a maximum of 16,000 acre feet per year from the lake's tributaries, even in wet years. This is approximately one-fifth of the amount formerly taken.

Around the shoreline efforts are being made to restore brackish lagoons and freshwater wetlands where springs and streams flow into the lake. It is hoped that a million or more teals, mallards, canvasbacks, pintails and other ducks and geese will again stop off at Mono as they did a century ago during their migrations. Gulls and shorebirds already dot its surface by the tens of thousands.

The California State Water Resources Control Board is making most of the decisions that are restoring the lake and its tributaries. The board actually sealed victories for groups such as the Mono Lake Committee, the Audubon Society, Ducks Unlimited and California Trout.

The water rights actions of Los Angeles probably were a blessing in disguise, however, and the return of water by Los Angeles has fostered a new attitude among some experts. By halting development in the Owens Valley, "Los Angeles saved this region," according to G. Mathias Kondolf, associate professor of environmental planning at the University of California at Berkeley. "The net result has been about as good as you could possibly hope for. If Los Angeles had not taken the water, this place would look like Bakersfield."

The area's national forests already have more recreational visitors for skiing, hiking and fishing than the Grand Canyon, Yellowstone and Glacier national parks combined. The revived streams—and Mono Lake—will only increase tourist interest, although the ecosystem can never be restored to its condition when the Paiute Indians were the only humans to inhabit the area.[6]

FOOTNOTES — CHAPTER 5

1. Israel C. Russell, "Quaternary History of Mono Valley, California," U.S.G.S. 1883, pages 271, 279, fifth annual report.
2. Bodie Standard News, August 23, 1880.
3. Israel C. Russell, "Quaternary History of Mono Valley, California," page 296.
4. J. Ross Browne, "A Trip to Bodie Bluff in 1883," page 63.
5. Mark Twain, "Roughing It," pages 243, 245.
6. San Francisco Chronicle, Nov. 26, 1995

CHAPTER 6

FROM BILL BODEY TO BODIE BILL: OR "A HOT TIME IN THE OLD TOWN"

Today's visitor to the old ghost town of Bodie, California can credit a dish of ice cream or perhaps even a dish of red Jell-O for the buildings that stand there today.

The Bodie that exists today is what is left of a far larger town that stood until June 23, 1932—a hot, dry windy day—the day fire swept through a good many of the old structures, including most of the main street. The blaze destroyed three-fourths of Bodie. It was the third of three fires to strike the town from the time of its founding in the 1850s and was by far the most disastrous. It began on a hot afternoon just the day before school vacation was to begin.

LITTLE "BODIE BILL:" Photographed in 1932 by his mother, with the "Bon Ton" school in the background, which was spared in the 1932 fire. Bill was 2 years, 9 months old. (From the Millslagle collection)

Unlike the town's two earlier fires this one occurred when Bodie was sparsely populated since most mining activities by 1932 had been abandoned. Few residents remained to rebuild, nor was there any necessity. And so, the Bodie seen today is the Bodie that has stood since the Great Depression.

Did little "Bodie Bill," really start that fire? Newspaper accounts of the day had citizens placing the blame on a small boy supposedly playing with matches. Some called him "Bodie Bill." Publications even carried photographs of a toddler in bib overhauls holding a garden hose and even under one photo the caption reads:

"'BODIE BILL', THE BOY WHO STARTED THE 1932 FIRE BEHIND THE SAWDUST CORNER SALOON"

Another reads:

"'BODIE BILL', THE FIREBUG WHO SET BODIE ON FIRE"

For more than six years the authors searched and researched to determine the true identity of the toddler in overhauls and whether he actually started the fire and specifically to put an end to conjecture of more than 60 years in which the public was led to believe, based on hearsay, that the little boy in the photos did spark the blaze that burned Bodie in 1932.

And the mystery was solved. The mother of our toddler had written and had, herself, published a 40-page booklet which she entitled, "BODIE BILL."

With the aid of the booklet, and by obtaining additional facts from family members and friends found through research, the "Bodie Bill" puzzle has ended.

Little "Bodie Bill" did exist and he did strike the match that ignited the 1932 fire. It was determined that he was lucky to escape the flames and research included several interviews—two with acquaintances of the mysterious little boy including one person who was with Bill that day in 1932, just minutes before the fire turned the old Sawdust Corner Saloon and most of the town into an inferno.

Whether this child, not yet three years of age, started the fire intentionally probably will never be determined. His identity is positive, however.

The search for little Bill extended from 1988 to 1994. It was aided by discovery of the surname "Godward" uncovered in two publications, the first of which was a yellowed August, 1944 issue of "The Pony Express," an obscure Placerville, California monthly tabloid that boasted its contents were based upon "True Stories of Famous Frontier Trails."[1]

The second reference to the surname "Godward" was found in a book written by Margaret Elizabeth Currie Calhoun entitled "Pioneers of Mono Basin." Mrs. Calhoun was born in 1889 on the old J.G. Thompson Ranch just a quarter-mile from Mono Lake and twenty miles from Bodie.

"The Pony Express" story included a second photo of "Bodie Bill" in bib overhauls. The caption beneath states:

LITTLE BODIE BILL: This photo, often called "The Firebug Who Set Bodie On Fire" was widely circulated in the 1930's, and even found its way onto a postcard which Bill's mother stopped with a court order. (From the Frank & Joan Millslagle collection)

"THIS YOUNG LAD IN BIB OVERHAULS COULD TELL YOU A LOT ABOUT BODIE IF ONE COULD NOW FIND HIM. HIS MOTHER CLAIMED TO BE CANARY JANE FROM THE WILD BAD LANDS OF DAKOTA, WHO DROVE A FOUR HORSE TEAM WITH LINES BETWEEN HER HUSKY TEETH AND FIRED A PISTOL WITH BOTH HANDS."

The second photo apparently was taken at the same time and location as the first, probably by Bill's mother. The background in The Pony Express photo shows Bodie School, but the caption incorrectly identifies it as a church.

Had The Pony Express writer in that year 1944 taken time to do some research, he would have discovered that his little "firebug" was just over the

Sierra Nevada Mountains in Reno, Nevada, attending Reno High School and doing summer work in a gas station, and he also would have found that Bill's mother, whom the newspaper referred to as "Canary Jane," was a cook and a housewife, also in that "Biggest Little City in the World."

As for Mrs. Calhoun, she wrote about the 1932 fire: "…A little boy, two and a half years old, by the name of Billy Godward, was playing with matches and caused the fire of 1932, burning most of Main Street. Some questioned Billy's doing this as he was so young, and some people never believed it was his fault."[2]

A GHOST TOWN IN FLAMES: Just a matter of minutes after a little
boy, not yet three years of age, who was playing with matches, set fire to
the Sawdust Corner Saloon, Bodie's main street was in flames. The Bodie
Club, in the foreground, was one of the first buildings
to burn on that hot day, June 23, 1932.
(From the Millslagle collection)

Beyond this point the trail of information involving the Godward name came to an abrupt halt. But the search took on a new life when a friend of the authors, John Holt of Bishop, California, a Sierra town some 100 miles south of Bodie, in early 1994 observed a Reno newspaper column entitled, "Family Speaks in Defense of Bad Boy of Bodie." It referred to a previous column by the same writer who had repeated the story of the 1932 fire and little "Bodie Bill's" alleged involvement as a "firebug," but without mentioning the surname "Godward."[3]

One Frank Millslagle of Yerington, Nevada, whose wife, Joan, was a cousin of "Bodie Bill," had disputed the "firebug" connotation, suggesting instead that the 1932 fire might have been started "in an abandoned opium den."

HAPPY CADET: William Brewster Godward was a happy cadet when he entered Palo Alto Military Academy at the age of 11 in 1940.
(From the Millslagle collection)

MOTHER AND SON: Delcie and Bill are shown together when Bill returned home from the military academy at age 14. He was a student there from 1940 until he entered high school in Reno, Nevada.
(From the Millslagle collection)

The authors contacted the Millslagles. They agreed to an interview and the authors at last were able to determine heretofore unknown facts about WILLIAM BREWSTER GODWARD, alias "BODIE BILL."

FACT: William Brewster Godward was born in old St. Mary's Hospital in Reno, Nevada August 8, 1929. This was confirmed by a visit to the Washoe County Health Department where records are stored.

FACT: Bill's parents, now deceased, were William T. Godward, a Bodie mining engineer, and Delcie Pearl Millslagle Godward. Delcie operated a store and a hotel in Bodie and was a cook there at the time of her son's birth.

In 1965, Delcie wrote and had published several copies of a booklet. Bill's father had died by that time and she had remarried and signed the introduction, "Delcie P. LeMay nee Godward." According to Mrs. Millslagle, Delcie's second husband, Victor LeMay, was a cousin of the late U.S. Air Force General Curtis LeMay of Strategic Air Command fame. Victor later died in a mine cave-in in Prescott, Arizona.

Included in Delcie's booklet were excerpts of her life in Bodie, and in Carson City, Virginia City, Reno and Lovelock, Nevada, and vignettes regarding her son, Bill. She printed several photographs, copies of which are included in this publication. She stated little Bill was named after his father and that his middle name, Brewster, was the first name of the Reno Baptist Church minister, Brewster Adams, a good friend of Delcie and her husband, and the cleric who married them.

The Millslagles assisted in obtaining the only remaining copy of Delcie's booklet which was loaned to the authors by a surviving half-sister of Delcie's, Mrs. Muriel McMurtrey of Valentine, Nebraska, who was in her nineties.

Another family relative, Mrs. Wanda Biggs of Carson City, whose mother also was a half-sister of Delcie and Mrs. McMurtrey, assisted in contacting Mrs. McMurtrey and with the aid of Mrs. Biggs' daughter, Mrs. Laura Brown of Stockton, California, the booklet was delivered into the hands of the authors.[4]

Of course, the hope was, after all these years, to be able to interview William Brewster Godward, alias "Bodie Bill," who would have been 65 years of age. But this was not to be.

Tragically, "Bodie Bill" died at the age of 21, a day after suffering a broken back and other injuries in a January 25, 1951 single-car accident on Highway 395 near Susanville, California north of Reno. He and his wife of just 16 months, the former Dian Devereaux of Sandusky, Ohio were on a delayed honeymoon traveling to Portland, Oregon following a visit with Delcie in Arizona. Immediately after the accident he was flown to the Presidio in San Francisco where he died the following day in Marine Hospital.

BODIE BILL AND BRIDE: William Brewster Godward and his bride, the former Dian Devereaux of Sandusky, Ohio, were married only 16 months when Bill, 21, was fatally injured in an auto crash in 1951 near Susanville, California. (From the Millslagle collection)

His wife, who was uninjured in the crash, and his mother, were both at his bedside. At the time of his death, Bill had served five-and-a-half years in the United States Coast Guard and he was an Engineman Third Class. His stepfather had just recently been killed in the mining mishap. Delcie had been struck a double tragedy.

The body of William Brewster "Bodie Bill" Godward will forever rest in Golden Gate National Cemetery in San Bruno, California in Section N, Plot 2870.

Mentioned at the outset was a dish of ice cream and a dish of red Jell-O. The Reno newspaper article referred to a Mrs. Thelma Roebuck, 81, of Reno, and a native of Bodie. The authors contacted her and learned she was one of seven children of a former Mono County sheriff. She referred us to an older sister, Mrs. Loretta Gray, then 93, and Mrs. Gray's daughter, Mrs. Ferne Tracey, both of Oakland, California. Mother and daughter lived in Bodie at the time of the fire.

They were contacted and agreed to an interview—one which proved extremely informative since Mrs. Tracey not only was in Bodie at the time of the fire—she was attending an end-of-the-school-year party at the Bodie School with eight other children including William "Bodie Bill"

Godward. Little Bill was just 2 years and 10 months of age and had been dropped off at the school by his mother to attend the party.

AT THE BODIE SCHOOL PARTY: Mrs. Ferne Tracey (right) attended
the party that hot afternoon of June 23, 1932, when little Bodie Bill
Godward refused red Jell-O after expecting ice cream and as a result much
of Bodie was reduced to ashes. Mrs. Tracey is pictured at our interview
with her mother, the late Mrs. Loretta Gray.
(A Doug Brodie photo)

These are Mrs. Tracey's words:

"It was the end of the school year and a party was held to celebrate. I was nine and there were only about nine kids, and he was invited and his mom dropped him off. The party was over and they started serving dessert. They told him he was going to have ice cream, and he wanted ice cream and they served him Jell-O. It was red Jell-O. He got very angry and took off. I don't know whether the teacher (she later identified the teacher as Ella Cain) should have done anything, but she didn't, and he just ran home and his mom wasn't there, and he got some book matches. There was a saloon on the corner, and the street went up like this." Mrs. Tracey gestured to describe a hill.

"And there was a big building behind it…it was a vacant building and like the old buildings had, it had this cheese cloth hanging down, the kind you'd put paper over. It was a perfect spot for a fire and it was over.

"Somebody saw him. I don't remember who, and apparently he had the matches with him when his mom caught up with him. I think she'd been at the Post Office. I don't think she was at home."[5]

BODIE, PRIOR TO 1932 FIRE: Looking north on Main Street, just after a rain. Bodie was almost abandoned, but some gold mining of ore heaps continued with the assistance of James S. Cain. Little Bodie Bill was blamed for starting the fire. At its peak in 1879–80, population in Bodie hit 10,000. (By permission of Eastern California Museum)

Mrs. Tracey's description of the building that Bodie Bill set fire to was very much like his mother's description in her 1965 booklet: "The old deserted building with rafters of old lining and wallpaper blowing in the wind, were the perfect set-up for a fire added to this hazard. Our fire hoses had deteriorated so that when the crew unwound them they fell in pieces at each turn of the wheel. So Bridgeport, 35 miles away, came to us but not in time to do much good. The buildings in the center of the town burned down including my place, and in the cash drawer the silver all melted together in a conglomerate mess. The paper currency became cinders."

She added, "So many have asked and wondered what became of Bodie Bill, so the following is a resume of the very short life destiny had planned for him."

She wrote that the family was preparing to leave Bodie after the mine which employed Bill's father closed when the Treadwell-Yukon Co., which was reworking tailings from the many old mines, hired him as manager. As a result the family was able to remain in the town until after the 1932 fire. This firm also was forced to close, however, and the little family moved to Reno. Bill's father found a job in Virginia City and the family moved there. Delcie ran a hotel until school started and then took Bill to Carson City where she enrolled him in school. She and Bill remained there from 1933 until 1940 when she placed him in Palo Alto Military Academy in Palo Alto, California at age 11.

Delcie said she believed her son needed the companionship of a father which her husband was unable to provide because he was usually away working in a distant mine.

MAKING 1929 BODIE MOVIE: Pictured in front of the Sawdust Corner Saloon are several members of Universal Studios film crew. The studio used Bodie as "New Jerusalem" in its first Western filmed in sound, "Hells Heroes," which starred Charles Bickford and little Bodie Bill Godward, the boy who set fire to the town in 1932. (By permission of Eastern California Museum)

The events involving Bodie during the period after Bill's birth were recorded by Delcie in her booklet, with some needing correction and/or clarification. She had taken time off to go to the hospital in Reno. She wrote that two weeks later she returned to Bodie to find that the house she and her husband had been renting—known as the Hoover House, a dwelling once occupied by Theodore Hoover, brother of then President Herbert Hoover, when Theodore was superintendent of the Standard Mine—and most of the town of Bodie, had been temporarily taken over by Universal Studios, a Hollywood film company. Universal was filming a Western and Delcie referred to the film as "Hells Angels," which she said starred Jean Harlow and Charles Bickford.

Apparently tiny baby "Bodie Bill" also starred in the film. Referring to the two stars, she wrote: "They were the first to carry young William on their horses so he and our white fox terrier called Pinky were in the Hells Angels picture."

Again, Delcie had erred in her recollection. The authors determined the film "Hell's Angels" was a World War I aerial epic produced and directed by the late Howard Hughes and had no connection with Bodie. The film that was made in Bodie in 1929 was "Hell's Heroes" and did star Charles Bickford, but Jean Harlow was not in it.[6]

Delcie might have been correct in stating her baby Bill was in at least one scene. The picture was the third remake of a total of seven films based on the famous Peter B. Kyne novel, "The Three Godfathers," and was the first Western made on location by Universal to include sound. A photo in this publication includes the 1929 film crew. The story is based upon a bank robbery in the town of "New Jerusalem" and during their flight the three robbers find a dying mother and her baby on the trail. They promise the mother they will return the baby to New Jerusalem, which, of course, is actually Bodie.

Whether Bodie Bill is that baby is a matter of conjecture.

The Hoover House occupied by Delcie and her little family was saved from the 1932 fire and can be seen by today's visitor to Bodie. It stands adjacent the entrance to the Standard Mill, southwest of the end of Wood Street.

The Millslagles recalled that Delcie would become upset when she would hear the oft-repeated stories about her son starting the Bodie Fire. They recalled one instance, when she was informed a postcard was being sold bearing a bib overhauls photo of her son that described him as "BODIE BILL, THE FIREBUG WHO SET BODIE ON FIRE," that she obtained a court order halting sale of the cards.

Nowhere in our research were the authors able to determine that Delcie ever acknowledged or admitted her son actually started the 1932 fire.

Bill's mother was especially proud of a nine-stanza Christmas poem written to her by her son in letter form just before Christmas, 1945, following his admission into the U.S. Coast Guard. She had several copies printed and we have included it in this chapter, courtesy of Frank and Joan Millslagle.

Delcie concluded her Bodie Bill book with a copy of her son's Honorable Discharge from the Coast Guard, accompanied by a note from then Coast Guard Commandant Vice Admiral Merlin O'Neill, who stated it was offered "as a tribute to your son's sacrifice in the service of his country."

"So," Delcie concludes, "this is just one small episode of a great mining district which was a mediocre producer (again she was in error) but yet made a few very rich men among them J.S. Cain, the owner at the time of the fire. Even his bank which burned had a fire proof safe, and the contents were not burned. It was amusing to see the larger boys and yes, some adults, descend on the burned wood floor of the bank, each one getting a pouch of pure mining gold that had spilled on the weigh-in of the dust. It was quite lucrative for these lads and excitement ran high as they spent and respent their ill-gotten gains."

BODIE BILL AND BUDDY: Bodie Bill Godward, 9 (left) and
friend George Groth, who lives in Carson City, were photographed
together in May of 1938, when Bill was a Carson City resident
with his mother. He told of setting the 1932 Bodie fire. INSET;
George Groth as he appears today at his Carson City home.
(Courtesy of George Groth)

Further research assisted the authors in piecing together other events in the short life of Bodie Bill. Delcie wrote that her son joined the Coast Guard on his 17th birthday, August 8, 1945, when actually this was his 16th birthday. She signed parental consent papers stating he was 17.

"...with all the war news and talk going on, he began to speak of going in the Coast Guard. At first I thought it was something he'd outgrow, but as his 17th birthday rolled around he was more adamant, so I journeyed with him to Alameda, California, where to his delight he was admitted. He was short one year of high school . . ."

Two Stockton, California sisters, Mrs. Joan Remington and Mrs. Moss Pickering, former Carson City, Nevada residents, and, with Mrs. Biggs, elementary school students in the Nevada state capitol during the 1930s, aided in our research. All three women attended a 1994 Carson City High School reunion. The two Stockton women had remembered a small boy joining their classes in elementary school in the 1930s, and that he had told of "setting fire to Bodie."

They assisted the authors in contacting a childhood friend and member of the high school reunion, George Groth. As a boy in the 1930s, Groth spent many hours playing with William Brewster (Bodie Bill) Godward. Groth said he lived just around the block from Sunset Court, a Carson City motel operated by Delcie. He and Bill were nine or ten years of age. Groth recalled that Bill told him of the 1932 fire and that he had started it while playing with matches. Groth said the two of them would often roast potatoes in a bonfire and that Bill would describe the event while they waited for their potatoes to cook. "He told me his mother really paddled him good when she found out what he had done."[7]

Groth, who resides in Carson City, is no stranger to Bodie. His grandfather was George Gilson, a Bodie pioneer and partner in Gilson-Barber & Co., a well known early-day general merchandise store. Gilson was a member of the group of Bodie businessmen who unearthed William Bodey's bones in 1879, twenty years after the town's namesake had been buried on the trail where he died during the winter of 1859.

The 1932 fire was described in that year's June 30 Inyo Register in Bishop, a week later:

"What was left of Bodie was almost wiped out by fire last Thursday afternoon. Press reports assert that a child playing with matches started the conflagration. Whatever the origin, it began at the rear of the Sawdust Saloon and spread rapidly from one building to another. Most of the men were working in the mines; those in town got out the hose lines. It is said that a couple of ladies also assisted in getting out the hose. But the water system was clogged because of the breakage of a screen which allowed debris to enter the pipes, and no headway could be made against the destruction of the dry wooden buildings.

"Old landmarks, including buildings which had escaped from the two

disastrous fires of earlier history, were swept away, 14 in all being burned
...until only five buildings remained in the business section, and very few
on the borders. Chief among the lost structures was the Bodie Bank, the
property of J.S. Cain, Bodie's grand old man, who had stayed with the
old camp through bonanza and borrasco. His building, in which millions
of dollars were handled in the past, housed a collection of souvenirs and
relics of much historic value; whether there was any salvage is unknown.
Mr. Cain was the chief loser in the conflagration, he owning a number of
the burned structures...with the withdrawal of Treadwell-Yukon Co.
from production, it would seem that this blow may be final. The burning of Bodie is a disaster to the historically minded more than to the production of the mining world."[8]

WILLIAM BREWSTER GODWARD: Engineman Third Class,
United State Coast Guard. (From the Millslagle collection)

Forty years earlier, in 1892, Bodie had suffered its second major fire
when flames broke out in the kitchen of Mrs. Perry's Restaurant. Water
mains initially failed the firefighters, too. A valve near the Standard Mill
had been turned off. When it was finally opened, firefighters were able to
douse the flames, but only after extensive damage had resulted. The town
was thriving and back street buildings were moved up to Main Street to
fill in the gaps.

Bodie's first major fire occurred during the summer of 1884 as a result of a drunken miner stumbling through the front window of the Stewart & Brothers Drug Store. A burning lamp overturned igniting spilled oil and the building was destroyed.

The newly formed Bodie Water Co. had installed a hydrant system in 1879 and it proved to be in working order. The Bodie Fire Department, organized the following year, 1880, responded but when the hoses were hooked up, only a dribble was evidenced. After a frantic search to determine the trouble, it was found the pump in the Lent Shaft was not operating and when it was turned on, water poured into the reservoir and on through the hoses. The fire was soon out and the town was saved.

Billeb noted in his book: "The volunteer fire department was organized and equipped with handdrawn hose carts. The equipment should have been ample to handle almost any fire, but in both of Bodie's big conflagrations troubles developed which seriously hampered firefighting. Reservoir screens were clogged and the volunteers failed to understand the function of the left-handed British hydrants which were wrenched and jammed shut instead of open."[9]

FINAL RESTING PLACE: The body of William Brewster "Bodie Bill" Godward rests forever in Golden Gate National Cemetery in San Bruno, California, Section N, Plot 2870. (A Doug Brodie photo)

Dedicated To My Mother—Mrs. D.P. Godward

Well now that I'm in the Coast Guard Mom,
I don't have any say.
In fact the admirals tell me just
What to do each day.

They won't give me a leave for
Christmas so it seems,
But we've got them beat there Mom,
I'll be there if only in my dreams.

True, this is the first Christmas
That we've ever been apart,
So when I say that I'll think of you that day—
It comes right from my heart.

I guess I never realized how much Christmas meant
Until I found myself away from home,
So I decided I'd let you know how much it means,
By writing this little poem.

I remember our little tree in the window,
And the lights throwing off all a merry glow,
And under the tree were presents
From all those we love and know.

I remember all the fun I had
Handing the packages out—
I used to save yours till last,
Just to watch you pout!

I recall the presents—one from dad—
Oh—and one from Uncle Bert too—
But the present I'll always be looking for,
Is the one that comes from you.

Well Mom, I've had a lot of fun
Recalling all those times again.
Next time we get together,
It will probably start out— "remember when"

Well I'll close this poem for now Mom,
This poem between you and me,
And I pray that today and every day,
God will watch over thee.

Your Loving Son,[10]

BILL

FOOTNOTES — CHAPTER 6

1. Lavender, Pony Express, August 1944
2. Margaret Calhoun, "Pioneers of Mono Basin," page 81
3. Reno Gazette Journal, February 21, 1994
4. Delcie P. LeMay, "Bodie Bill"
5. Mrs. Ferne Tracey, an interview
6. J. Robert Nash and Stanley Ralph Ross, "The Motion Picture Guide, H-K, 1927-1983," page 142
7. George Groth, an interview
8. Inyo Register, June 30, 1932
9. Billeb, page 149
10. A poem by Bodie Bill Godward

CHAPTER 7

BODIE'S SCOURGE—A CITY OF THE DEAD

The year 1879 in Bodie proved not only to be the town's most prolific in terms of growth, but its worst in terms of pneumonia victims. For whatever reason, and there seemed to be as many as there were citizens in Bodie, pneumonia was responsible for many deaths, especially during that fateful winter.

COVERED BY SNOW: The extreme winter cold was said to be responsible for pneumonia epidemics in Bodie. This is a photo of modern day Bodie during winter. Snow often buried the town with depths of 15 to 20 feet. (A Jim Watson photo)

Pneumonia struck the male population the hardest, and most often. Usually the victim was a miner. Some said their lungs could not stand the combination of hot, humid, often dusty air in the mines, followed by extremely cold, dry air when they emerged out into the open, combined with the altitude—a mile and a half up. And that this would be especially difficult to handle if the miner might already have a respiratory problem, and might be a smoker.

From the Mammoth City Times newspaper of October 15, 1879 is this story placed next to a listing of deaths of five Bodie men—all pneumonia victims: "The prevalence of pneumonia in Bodie is something alarming. The deaths average fully one a day, and the disease seems on the increase. One peculiar feature of pneumonia in Bodie is its fatality. Once it gets hold on the patient, recovery is well nigh impossible. Physicians say that the cause of it is the hard, dry light atmosphere, which when the disease has full headway makes the work of breathing so painful as to actually exhaust the sufferer's strength.

"Here in Mammoth, we have no sickness whatever. We do not now recall a single case of pneumonia, or indeed any lung complaint. Though higher in altitude than Bodie, the air here is charged with moisture from the forest and lakes, and there is also something no doubt in the odor from the Spruce (there are no spruce in the Mammoth area) and fir, and which has a good effect upon the lungs. Mammoth City is one of the healthiest places in California."[1]

The following month the paper carried an article entitled: "BODIE'S SCOURGE (giving Mammoth another pat on the back): There is something appalling in the magnitude of the death rate in Bodie from pneumonia. During the past month it is believed over 100 deaths have occurred from that disease alone. The Bodie papers have hitherto kept discreetly silent as to its ravages, even going so far as to omit the usual death notices. But now the secret can be no longer kept. We observe in the 'News' of the 11th, published under the regular head of 'DEATHS,' no less than six fatal cases of pneumonia.

"A Catholic clergyman being sent for from Mammoth City to administer to a sick man here, replied that it was utterly impossible for him to come; that his time was taken up day and night, at the bedside of pneumonia patients. That during the past four weeks he had witnessed the death struggle of over thirty victims of the dread disease. The Bodie people are determined to attribute the cause of such fatality to some remediable agent, and therefore lay it to the condition of the water and the streets, but this is clearly wrong.

"The condition of the streets has but little to do with it in the opinion of the best physicians. The real cause lies in the hard, dry, biting cold atmosphere of Bodie, which renders a genuine case of pneumonia almost impossible to cure. Here in Mammoth we are especially favored. Though higher in altitude than Bodie, there is a moisture in the air from our lakes and forests which effectually wards off the fell destroyer."[2]

The Bodie Standard of November 11, 1879 corroborated reports about Bodie pneumonia deaths carried in other newspapers. The Mammoth paper carried this story copied from the Bodie newspaper, and again headed it "THE BODIE SCOURGE—Our reporter interviewed one of our physicians this morning in regard to this dire disease and obtained some very valuable information. He stated that the recent fall of snow, coming as it did, was in nine cases out of ten fatal to those who were sick at the time. There is no use concealing the fact—pneumonia prevails at an alarming extent at the present time in our midst. This morning, Dr. Robinson was called upon to visit three new cases, all of whom the doctor states were very bad.

"Mr. Anderson of the O.K. Barber Shop, the proprietor of the Empire Saloon and the other a stranger. There was a report that there were seven dead bodies brought to the dead house last night." (This is the brick building with the northwest corner missing, located at the edge of the Bodie Cemetery and listed in the Park brochure as "Old Morgue" in which bodies were stored, usually in the winter, until they could be buried. The ground would be frozen and dynamite used to blow a hole in the earth if a winter interment was a necessity.)

"A representative of the 'Standard' visited the dead house this morning and found only four, all of whom were mentioned in yesterday's Standard, only two deaths, as far as we could learn having taken place last night."[3]

Four days later the Mammoth City Times carried this story: "BEHIND THE SCENES—The Virginia City Enterprise has received the foregoing remarkable letter:

" 'Bodie, Mono Co., Cal. Nov. 13, 1879. Editor Enterprise: Bodie has boasted of her generosity.

A TYPICAL BODIE GRAVESITE: This survivor of the past has long
since parted with its old wooden marker. The intricate wrought iron facade
is one of many remaining in the Bodie Cemetery. (A Jim Watson photo)

"'She has a test before her now today. There are twelve dead bodies in
the town, four of which were poor men. They have been lying in Mr.
Ward's (the local mortuary) since last Monday for lack of someone to put
up for a small pine box. The city authorities say they will not bury them.
The County refuses, and Dr. Summers, the County Hospital agent,
refuses. For God's sake send us over a few extra boxes. I expect to see these
men rolled in blankets and dumped into some old shaft soon. Our papers
do not chronicle one-half the deaths here. The deaths appear to all be in
the middle and lower part of town. When Mr. Daly said there were five
deaths per day he was as near right as any newspaper has reported from
here. I am an old Comstock miner and I have never seen old Virginia
refuse any one a decent burial. (signed) J.D.J.' " [4]

And on it went. The Mammoth City paper November 15: "Private
letters continue to be received in Mammoth, stating that the newspapers
in Bodie do not tell the half about the pneumonia, and are endeavoring
to conceal the real facts. It seems to us that is bad policy. Tell the truth,
gentlemen, always. It is better in the end." [5]

Warren Loose devotes some lines in his book to the "scourge" of 1879,
and also refers to it as the "siege" and the "plague."

"As the busy days of late fall arrived the camp was subjected to a siege
of pneumonia, or typhoid pneumonia as it was sometimes called. Many
of its citizens were laid low with this malady. Although some did not survive the plague (as the Virginia Enterprise called it), the number of deaths
was grossly exaggerated. One writer in the same paper dashed off a well-
varnished account that claimed the people in Bodie were 'dying like

sheep' without medical attention; and are not given a decent burial; and he expected, that men will be rolled up in blankets and dumped into some old mine shaft soon."

Loose apparently was referring to the aforementioned letter and he added a quote from the Enterprise:

EARLY DAY HEARSE: This horse-drawn hearse is pictured in front of the Bodie "Dead House" at the edge of the Bodie Cemetery. This hearse is now located in the Bodie museum. (A Jim Watson photo)

"No less an authority than Bodie undertaker H. Ward was called upon to refute the rash of absurd stories making the pages of the outside press. This worthy statistician of the marble orchard penned a hasty last-minute census of citizens who had recently answered the toot of Gabriel's horn."[6]

Ward's letter:

"Permit me, through your paper, to correct some misrepresentations which I read in the Enterprise of Sunday, November 13, headed A SHOCKING CONDITION OF THINGS IN BODIE. In the first place, there never have been 12 dead bodies buried in Bodie at one time since I have been here the last two years. The most at any time was seven. The last month, October, there were 29 deaths. I buried them all myself, except one. That one was sent below for interment. In the present month, November, up to the 17th, there have been 20 deaths all told, of which I will give you the names and dates for publication if you desire."

The Enterprise story continued:

"However, the (Bodie) Daily Standard of the eighteenth, which published embalmer Ward's tally sheet, came forth with, 'The boys don't swing the 'hurdies' to any great extent in these funeral times of Pneumonia'," and followed this comment with another flip literary jab:

"A dog was run over in the Main Street by a wagon the other day, and killed. We mention this fact for fear that some of the outside papers might get hold of it and say that the dogs of Bodie are dying of Pneumonia, and that the papers are keeping it a secret."

From the Bodie Standard of November 9, 1880 came this sarcastic comment: "It was almost a year later that a thoughtful scribe after considerable meditation on the real cause of the outbreak of sickness that fall, hit the nail on the head with the sage observation that 'It is a well known fact that the wells of Bodie are simply receptacles of the drainage of surrounding outhouses and surface filth. The water is so obnoxious as to be unfit for any use and is a certain source of dissemination of disease'."[7]

The Reno Weekly Gazette employed a correspondent in 1879 whose byline was "Honest Miner." In an article he wrote June 17, he referred to pneumonia in Bodie as follows:

"I only know one place where the climate is likely to be more disagreeable, and that is the sulphury regions…the climate of Bodie seems to be very unhealthy especially for men. Yet there are over 300 children here and they seem to enjoy the best of health. Ladies also are seldom sick. In the past 15 months only 4 women and 1 child have been buried, while for many weeks there has been a funeral every day. The enemy is pneumonia which attacks the strongest men in preference to the sickly or the weak.

"The air is light and cold, the men who became overheated are chilled almost instantly, unless extraordinary precautions are taken and their lungs have to bear the whole shock."[8]

A story of the opposite nature appeared in the Reno Weekly Gazette November 10, 1879:

"A TRIP TO BODIE—L.P. Walker recently returned from a trip to Bodie and Aurora. He states reports about pneumonia in Bodie have been much exaggerated. The victims to the disease are commonly men who get drunk and lie about the streets or those who expose themselves to sudden chills. With proper precautions no one need fear pneumonia."

"Mr. Walker desires to warn everyone going to Bodie against the fatal effects of drinking whiskey. The fumes of the whiskey, he thinks, combined with the rarity of the air or the low temperature and/or dust, or mingle with the elevation of the ozone, or somehow in a way that owing to the extreme dryness of the atmosphere may be perhaps be mitigated it is still apt to produce a degree of mental exhilaration that should be or at least is in great part due to peculiar climactic conditions that surround, so to speak, in a region the somewhat anomalous state of the site of low civilization of the camp."[9]

It would appear that with his command of the English language, Mr. Walker has summed up the entire situation in the Gazette story.

From the November 12, 1879 Mammoth City Times comes an unusual story of one of the many pneumonia deaths, followed up by news reports of action taken by the Mono County coroner's jury and eventually the County Grand Jury.

"Mark Parnell died the other day in Bodie of pneumonia. The circumstances of the death were such that the coroner held an inquest and the jury returned a verdict that the death was caused by pneumonia aggravated by gross neglect of the County Physician…Dr. Summers and his son, who permitted the patient to be in a cold room, without change of clothes or the slightest care or comfort, other than the administration of a few medicines—no doubt reluctantly given.

"Mono County has long been disgraced by the inefficiency of its hospital management, but there has been no such glaring instance of incompetency and heartlessness than this. By the way, this Dr. Summers is the same who has recently been appointed public administrator. County physician and public administrator! May God save the poor man's life in the first place, but if he must die, may heaven have mercy upon his estate!"[10]

Parnell did not die in the County Hospital proper, but rather in the Magnolia Lodging House after initial treatment by Dr. Summers. The physician informed the Coroner's Jury he "has paid out over $1,000 for the accommodation of indigent sick outside of the hospital," according to the news story. The newspaper added:

"In Inyo County (the adjoining county to the south) there is a committee of citizens in different parts of the county whose duty it is to furnish the patient with a letter admitting him to the hospital. A contract is let to the lowest bidder at a stated figure. No applicant was ever turned away and the supervisors keep a jealous eye on the treatment of the patients. Such would be the only wise course for our board to pursue, and in case the hospital is over-crowded, let them act at once and in some way provide for the unfortunates."[11]

The Bodie Standard followed up on this suggestion with a demand that the Mono County Board of Supervisors instigate an investigation of the management of the Mono County Hospital and its administration, stating: "The testimony deduced showed that criminal negligence was the direct cause of the unfortunate man's death."

The situation involved unusual circumstances in that a county hospital had been constructed in May, 1878. It was a large two-story frame building. It gradually built up a patient load largely as a result of the high incidence of pneumonia victims in Bodie. As space became short, pneumonia victims were being placed in the same ward with patients suffering from tuberculosis, or, as they termed it then, consumption. As a result of the overcrowding and resulting shortage of hospital beds, patients were housed in lodging houses and hotels such as the Magnolia Lodging House in which Parnell died. Mono County contracted out for these facilities and the resultant high costs of treating the many patients led to the Board of Supervisors levying a $3 "Hospital Tax" on the county taxpayers.

The Bodie Standard commented: "We trust that Dr. Summers will come forward with a statement of what the hospital tax of three dollars paid by the largely increased population aggregates; what his expenses amount to in conducting the hospital, and in short, a practical account of his responsible charge...Mr. Summers states that the hospital has been running eighteen months and that but two patient have died. This certainly speaks well for the management, but it don't clear up the question."[12]

In May of 1879, six months prior to Parnell's death, the Grand Jury had investigated the hospital management and its handling of indigents because of increasing complaints. It maintained that no one should be turned away. Because of the handling of Parnell's case, Dr. Summers was charged with "gross neglect." This led to the formation of a Mono County Medical Society by Bodie's doctors at the end of November.

The Mono County Grand Jury that May had also stated the County Hospital was a "disgrace to the county." The jury found Dr. Summers and a Dr. Blackwood had not complied with their contract to operate the facility and had neglected to provide proper bedding, beds, hospital furniture and appurtenances for patients and had ignored sanitary regulations. The Board of Supervisors was advised at that time to withhold further payment to the physicians. Dr. Summers continued as hospital administrator.

The Bodie Chronicle June 17, 1879 had stated editorially—five months prior to the Grand Jury Action:

"The facts are that the jail is a better place than the hospital and the contractors ignored about everything, except their pockets; that the comforts of their victims were of the least consequence, money evidently, being their god."[13]

The operation of the hospital continued to be a problem. The Board of Supervisors launched another inquiry in 1881. Patient neglect was found, but not to the extent that Dr. Summers' contract was cancelled.

An item from the Mammoth City Times of October 18, 1879:

"A NICE PLACE TO LIVE—Bodieites are suffering from the ravages of pneumonia, and the daily death rate is becoming alarming. Three funerals in one day, and two more to follow on the next, and a little sandwiching in of the revolver once in a while, and their city of the dead will soon become of vast content."[14]

FOOTNOTES — CHAPTER 7

1. Mammoth City Times, October 15, 1879

2. Ibid, November 12, 1879

3. Bodie Standard, November 11, 1879

4. Mammoth City Times, November 15, 1879

5. Ibid, November 15, 1879

6. Loose, pages 108, 109

7. Bodie Daily Standard, November 18, 1879

8. Reno Weekly Gazette, June 17, 1879

9. Ibid, November 10, 1879

10. Mammoth City Times, November 12, 1879

11. Ibid, November 12, 1879

12. Bodie Standard, July 29, 1878

13. Bodie Chronicle, June 17, 1879

14. Mammoth City Times, October 18, 1879

CHAPTER 8

A RAILROAD . . . OR TWO

Mining developments were rapid in the years 1879 and 1880 and by 1881 it was obvious the boom town of Bodie needed improved means of transportation as hundreds of wagons delivered goods, materials and passengers daily, and toted that precious cargo of gold and silver to the outer world. (They say the only other cargo hauled out of Bodie was beer of excellent quality from seven breweries in Bodie, outstanding, the experts said, due to the purity of the Bodie spring water tapped from sources in the hills above the town.)

Word spread that a railroad might be coming. The nearby Mammoth City Times, in its Wednesday, November 5, 1879 edition, carried this story: "A RAILROAD TO BODIE—AN IMPORTANT MOVE BY THE VIRGINIA AND TRUCKEE RAILROAD CO.— We have good news to publish today; news which should be hailed with pleasure by every man who depends upon manual labor for a livelihood or who sympathizes with those who toil. Mr. D. O. Mills, who is at present in New York, has negotiated for the material necessary to extend the Virginia and Truckee Railroad...toward Bodie sixty miles, and the order has been, or will be in a day or two, given for the ties."[1]

AN 1887 RAILROAD PASS: Signed by Thomas Holt, general superintendent of the Bodie & Benton Railway and Commercial Co., this pass allowed George T. Mills, auditor of the "V&T&C&CRR" to travel on the Bodie line. The initials stood for "Virginia & Truckee & Carson & Colorado Railroad." (A Jim Watson photo)

It told of the virtues of such an endeavor, that it would open up the country to development and mining and "give active work to 4,000 more miners" and increase the farming population by at least 800 families.

The newspaper editorially lauded the plans of Mills, stating: "This is good news…we are rather inclined to believe that the certainty of the construction of the new wagon road across the mountains to Mammoth City may have had something to do with this sudden change of front."

The Mammoth City paper carried another story taken from the near-by Sutro Independent in which that paper, too, supported the plans for a railroad. "Why the matter has been put off this long we are at a loss to know…perhaps the railroad company in question is dubious as to the permanency of Bodie."

Of course, as it turned out, the latter point was well taken because Bodie began its decline in 1882. There was hesitation, however, and the Mammoth City Times in its October 10, 1879 edition wrote: "There is much opposition to the building of a railroad to Bodie among the people of Carson, because they derive great benefit from the teamsters, travelers, etc., who are compelled to remain over at that place, and because if the road is started it will not be directly from Carson, but from a point some six miles distant at a point on the Virginia and Truckee Railroad. The Carsonites have a pretty good time of it now…and they, directly and indirectly, levy tribute on Bodie and Mammoth freight with an exactness that does their love of gain credit."[2]

The Mammoth newspaper commented on a news story that appeared that week in the Virginia City Enterprise stating "that iron and ties have been ordered for a new railroad to Bodie, and that the work of building it will be begun by the Virginia and Truckee Company at once."[3]

The publication supported the idea, while, at the same time, hinting that Mills' proposal was probably being pushed because of plans for a new wagon road across the mountains to Mammoth City. "The building of such a road would make a railroad to Bodie an absolute necessity if the V. & T. R.R. Co. hope to retain their share of the carrying trade into Mono County. On the other hand, the railroad project is not likely to discourage or retard the plans of the wagon road builders. The latter will come through any how, and we in Mammoth will be entirely independent of Mr. Mills and his rails, for by the road we shall be able to land freight from San Francisco just as cheap, if not cheaper, than he can put it down here. However, we rejoice that the railroad is to be built, and hope that it will be pushed through with vigor."

Of course a railroad did come to Bodie. The booming mining town was using wood at a prodigious rate, consuming lumber for construction of stamp mills, mining supports, commercial buildings and dwellings, and cordwood for the all-consuming boiler furnaces to operate the mills, and for heating purposes. The hills and mountains immediately surrounding Bodie were barren, but 32 miles to the south lay thousands of acres of timbered mountainsides near Mono Lake.

In 1881 the Bodie Railway & Lumber Co. was organized. Articles of incorporation were filed January 16, 1881 and the directors listed were H. M. Yerington (for whom Yerington, Nevada was later named), A.J. Ralston, R.M. Graves, W.S. Woods, W. Willis, J.B. Low and J.M. Quay, with capital listed at one million dollars. The purpose of the railroad, the papers stated, was to "bring wood from the vicinity of Mono Lake for the Bodie market." As a result, a three-foot narrow gauge line extending from Bodie to Mono Saw Mills south of Mono Lake was constructed. The last spike was driven November 14, 1881. It was an immediate success, so much so the company planned an extension from Warm Springs Station on the east side of Mono Lake to Benton. It was announced a connecting line would be laid to join with the narrow gauge Carson & Colorado Railroad, being built by the aforementioned Mr. Mills. This would have resulted in a Bodie rail line to outside markets by rail connections to major cities.

The name of the Bodie line, therefore, was changed to Bodie & Benton Railway & Commercial Co. Nine miles of the line to Benton was graded when work suddenly halted without explanation. As a result, Bodie remained isolated so far as the railroad was concerned.

This story was printed in the August 14, 1882 edition of the Bodie Evening Miner:

"RAILROAD BUILDING—A short time ago the grading on the Bodie and Benton Railway was stopped en route to Benton, and much disgusted were our people thereat, but matters are not so bad as we supposed. The company will build the road from Benton Junction, instead of from the Mono Lake end, as by so doing its rolling stock, rails, supplies, etc., can be received entirely by rail, making a great saving in time and money. The surveyors of the company are now in the field locating the route from Benton this way, and as soon as the route is selected, grading will be commenced and the road pushed to an early completion."[4]

Emil W. Billeb, hired in 1908 as superintendent of the railroad, probably came up with the answer as to why the Bodie extension never became a reality. He wrote:

"…But it was assumed that the Mills interests looked with disfavor on the competition this would bring to lumber mills they controlled in the Lake Tahoe area, since Mono Mills lumber shipped over the proposed connection could have undersold the Tahoe product that had to be hauled all the way down from Carson City on the Carson & Colorado Railroad."[5]

The author of the book "Railroads of Nevada and Eastern California," David F. Myrick, offers a possible second reason for cancellation of the project:

"Adequate reasons for the abandonment of the project never were stated publicly by anyone in authority, but local sages had their expressed opinions. Some contended that the Carson & Colorado was to blame, as its failure to obtain rails delayed the extension of their line over Mount Montgomery Pass to Benton, and there was no incentive to rush a Bodie & Benton connection to an unfinished railroad."[6]

Even in 1908, however, there were prospects of the short Bodie to Mono Mills line being expanded. Billeb explained that the line's fortunes rose and fell with the prosperity of the Bodie area mines, and when a new gold rush developed in the Tonopah and Goldfield, Nevada areas in the early 1900's, so did possibilities for the Bodie & Benton. The railroad property was taken over in 1906 by a syndicate headed by Charles E. Knox, president of the Montana-Tonopah Mining Co. The Mono Lake Railway & Lumber Co. was organized, the purpose of which was to build a broad gauge line from Mono Mills east to connect with the Tonopah & Goldfield Railroad at Sodaville. It would be able to provide lumber, poles, wood, lime and other supplies to the mines at Tonopah, Goldfield, and other camps in Southern Nevada, hence the hiring of Billeb as superintendent.

Billeb concludes his discussion relative to expansion with the statement: "As it turned out, the proposed broad gauge railroad to Sodaville was never built. The old narrow gauge line continued its isolated run between Bodie and Mono Mills. With the gradual closing of mines in the Bodie, Aurora, and Masonic areas, demand for lumber and cordwood diminished and the lumber company halted operations."[7] The advent of electricity from hydroelectric power plants built at the base of the Eastern

Sierra slopes also hastened the decline of the rail line. These power plants provided electricity to the mines and mills at rates much cheaper than the cost of wood-burning steam power which had been developed at the stamp mills and mines. To pay off indebtedness, the railroad finally was dismantled within a period of two months in the fall of 1918 and rails and equipment were shipped to San Francisco and sold for scrap.

BODIE'S RAILROAD DEPOT: The Bodie Railway & Lumber Company went into operation November 14, 1881 when a narrow gauge line extended 32 1/2 miles from Bodie south to Mono Mills "to bring wood from the vicinity of Mono Lake for the Bodie market." This is the Bodie Depot as it stands today on Bodie Bluff above the townsite. The name of the railroad the following year was changed to Bodie & Benton Railway & Commercial Company. (A Jim Watson photo)

Knox had tried to revive the line in 1907 and, for a while, the production of lumber and firewood at Mono Mills kept the line operating. The line's name in 1907 was shortened to "Mono Lake Railway" after Knox separated the rail and lumber operations. He offered several proposals to keep the business continuing. These included an expansion to the west beginning at Bodie and running northwesterly to Bridgeport to a point near Sonora Pass; the boring of a four-mile-long tunnel beneath the crest of the Sierra Nevada Mountains, and then incorporating the use of stagecoaches and freight wagons to close the gap for a connection with a proposed second railroad referred to by Myrick as the "Sierra Railway," thus forming an independent route to tidewater via the Sierra and Santa Fe railroads. Knox sought support from the Tonopah & Goldfield Railroad (he was a director of that company's board), but did not get it.

Knox then proposed extending a line at Mina, Nevada, 2-1/2 miles to Mina Canyon, via Whiskey Canyon to Mono Lake. This proposal also died, as did the rest of his plans and eventually the railroad between Bodie and Mono Mills.

Bodie's railroad dreams did not stop here. Occasionally in the press would be references to the possibilities of Bodie and the Eastern Sierra being connected to various other parts of the west by rail.

On March 16, 1881, just two months after the Bodie Railway & Lumber Co. filed papers of incorporation, similar papers were filed in San Francisco for another railroad. This was to be called the "California and Nevada Railroad." Plans called for construction of this narrow gauge line from San Francisco to Bridgeport: on to Bodie with a terminus at Dexter Wells, located east of Mono Lake, about 15 miles south of Bodie. Had this line been constructed as planned, Bodie most certainly would have been connected by rail to the outside world (this may have been the "Sierra Railway" to which Knox referred when he proposed a connection with the Santa Fe) and there would have been a railroad across Sonora Pass. This would have been a prodigious fete, even today, considering the difficulties encountered when rail lines conquered Donner Summit in the middle of the nineteenth century.[8]

Nevertheless, capital stock for the California and Nevada Railroad was subscribed to in the amount of $2,500,000 of which $250,000 was put up initially. The line was to extend 250 miles in length with the route to run through Modesto, Sonora, Calaveras Big Trees, up through Alpine County and on to Bridgeport and Bodie. Directors listed for this railroad were John T. Doris, A.J. Rhodes, J.A. Breigart, M. Miller, B.B. Miner, James McKingley and C.A. Livingstone.

The Bridgeport Chronicle-Union issue of April 23, 1881, stated: "...In the near future, however, Mono will be relieved by the advent of the California Narrow Gauge Railroad which will be pushed from Oakland to Dexter Wells via Bridgeport and Bodie, with the utmost dispatch. That the building of this road is a foregone conclusion, we cite the facts that last week 160,000 feet of lumber were landed at Oakland for the company and President Davis and the Board of Directors visited Modesto last week and assured the citizens that the road would be there to move this season's crops. This road will be 217 miles shorter to Bodie than via the Central Pacific and the Carson and Colorado roads. Without the annoyance of changing cars, and the 40-mile stage trip, passengers can make the trip to Bodie in less time than to Reno."[9]

Just exactly who "Davis" was, and where they derived the railroad's name as "California Narrow Gauge Railroad" was not determined, but the newspaper was definitely referring to the same line. A follow-up story October 22, correctly referred to it:

"Work is in progress on the California & Nevada narrow gauge railroad in Stanislaus County."[10] This was followed by another story datelined November 5, 1881: "The Central and Southern Pacific Railroad folks have organized a company to build a railroad from Modesto to Bodie. As it is proposed to take the route adopted by the California & Nevada Company, it looks very much like a bluff."[11]

It perhaps was a bluff to thwart the new "upstarts" in their endeavor. Loose notes that in November of 1881 two railroad companies dreamed of laying rails to Bodie.

"The Modesto and Tuolumne and Mono Railroad Company was incorporated with a capital stock of $5,000,000—50,000 shares of $100 each, of which 1,500 had been subscribed. Charles Crocker, A.M. Town and W.B. Huntington were among the directors. The road was to be 150 miles in length, running from the San Joaquin Branch of the Central Pacific Railroad, thence through Stanislaus County, Tuolumne County and Mono County to Bodie."[12]

This, of course, was the "company" formed to compete with the California and Nevada Railroad. The big money outweighed the small-timers and when the smaller company folded in the face of such a formidable opponent, the Central Pacific dropped its plans. As a result, no one has ever constructed a railroad over Sonora Pass.

Loose refers to the California-Nevada group as "the brainchild of an enthusiastic but rather modestly endowed group of railroad dreamers…their scheme was direct and simple—a railroad from Oakland via Stockton and across the Sierra to Bodie. The high-water mark of their efforts was an 1881 eyeball survey of a route running east from Sonora in Tuolumne County in a probing effort to stake out a right-of-way across the Sierra. They located five gaps or passes that would enable them to push a line easterly in search of what lay beyond the mountains. On November 24, 1881 their survey party located the easternmost pass attained that fall and dubbed it New Strawberry Pass at an elevation of 5,775 feet. They placed it about 1-1/2 miles more or less southwest from what is known as Patterson's Pass on the Mono Wagon Road. This, however, was the grand termination of this railroad to Bodie.[13]

Perhaps the bluff was on the part of the narrow gauge folks. Of course, as it turned out, no one built the proposed railroad across Sonora Pass. And thus ended Bodie's railroad history, with the exception of the old station that stands in the saddle up on Bodie Bluff just to the east of the old ghost town. It is now within the state historic park property on 550 acres formerly leased by the now defunct Bodie Consolidated Mining Co. The firm, for a short period, took tour groups to the top of the bluff area and through the old depot building. The park personnel now do this by special arrangement.

An 1881 story involving the construction of the rail line between Bodie and Mono Mills ran in the Bridgeport Chronicle-Union:

"THE CHINESE: The Bodie Railway and Lumber Co. innocently supposing it has a right, in common with others, to employ whom it thought proper, set about fifty Chinamen grading near Mono Lake, a portion not over-inviting as a field for the labor of white men; and, also, set white men at work at the Bodie terminus. But it appears there are men in Bodie who deny the right to employ other than their kind.

"We are opposed to Mongolian labor as much as those men, and also to those who combine to drive men from honest toil. Not one of them would pay one dollar per week to a white woman for washing, if a Chinaman would do the work for 50 cents, yet they would force others to.

"For the purpose of preventing the employment of other than white labor, a meeting was held in Bodie, and a committee of about fifty appointed to proceed to Mono Lake and drive the Chinamen off. On Wednesday it went to the lake, but found that the laborers had been removed to one of the islands, the company using the steamer and barges for that purpose, and there they are 'happy and content', idly, under pay and well-provisioned, watching the starving enemy on the main land— about thirty miles from base of doubtful supplies. In this case the railroad company is master of the field."

ORE CARS LEAVING A MINE TUNNEL: Cars similar to these were hauled by a legendary mule named "Old Tom" who would pull up to six ore cars, but refused to do his chores if he heard a seventh car being hooked up. Old Tom knew how to tell time, too. When he heard the noon whistle he stopped work and when the whistle blew at quitting time, he again halted his endeavors. (By permission of Eastern California Museum)

"The committee will return to Bodie footsore and hungry, and the Chinamen will resume work. Sheriff Showers was ready to promptly act in case of necessity."[14]

Because of competition of jobs, anti-Chinese sentiment was pervasive in much of California and Nevada in the late 1800's. This "news story" from the Bodie Evening Miner in the summer of 1882 was obviously slanted as to become an editorial comment, but it indicated the anti-Chinese feelings then prevalent:

"THAT DREADFUL MEETING—As THE MINER all along predicted, the intelligent men of Bodie assembled and quietly discussed the Chinese question. Miners' Union Hall was crowded, and much interest exhibited by those assembled. The meeting was addressed by such men as McDavitt, Stephens, McDonnell, Reddy (Pat Reddy, Bodie's most prominent lawyer and later elected to the California State Senate), Jackson and Burke. No one expects anything new to be advanced before a California audience on this serious matter. Nothing new can be advanced. The only question before the people of California is whether the limited provisions of the anti-Chinese Law can be enforced and how they, in their individual and collective capacity, can aid in ridding the State of this terrible curse.

"No definite plan of action was agreed on by the meeting, but a committee was appointed to submit a report at some subsequent meeting. We have heard it suggested on the street that the movement was gotten up here by the Miners' Union for a purpose of their own. We do not understand it to be any such thing. The Union has really the only available hall in town fitted for such a purpose, and the active men in that body are to be commended for their public spirit and liberality in furnishing the hall and giving shape to the contemplated assemblage. The idea of coercion meets with no favor in Bodie; but there is a popular sentiment here, as everywhere else in the State, which will teach heedless men to begin to draw the line of preference somewhat more gingerly between white labor and Chinese labor. As the matter stands, it is a gratification to be able to announce that the life of (a) Chinaman is in no more 'danger' in Bodie to-day than it would be if he were in his own dear, sweet, loved Hong Kong."[15]

FOOTNOTES — CHAPTER 8

1. Mammoth City Times, November 5, 1879
2. Ibid, October 10, 1879
3. Ibid, November 5, 1879
4. Bodie Evening Miner, August 14, 1882
5. Billeb, page 36
6. David F. Myrick, "Railroads of Nevada and Eastern California," page 311
7. Billeb, page 36
8. Bridgeport Chronicle-Union, March 26, 1881
9. Ibid, April 23, 1881
10. Ibid, October 22, 1881
11. Loose, pages 189, 190
12. Ibid, page 193d
13. Bridgeport Chronicle-Union, March 26, 1881
14. Bodie Evening Miner, December 12, 1881
15. Ibid, July, 1882

CHAPTER 9

BODIE'S "SUBURB"

Bodie's mysterious "suburb" was visited very little by park tourists before 1997. Until that year, the area was outside the state park boundary, up and over Bodie Bluff along Standard Hill at the 9,000-foot level. In 1880 the "suburb" consisted of over 100 structures, not including hoisting works and shops, none of which stands today. Other than artifacts on the ground and just below the surface and references to the area in news reports of that period, it's as if the "suburb" never existed. What actually happened to the buildings is unknown.

Suburb construction began in 1878 when the area along Standard Hill was called "High Peak." The suburb extended down the ridge and saddle to Silver Hill, to the southeast of Bodie.

A 550-acre area in which the suburb was a part, was purchased by the State of California and added to Bodie's State Historic Park in July of 1997. Additional information pertaining to the purchase is referred to in the final chapter.

Wedertz notes in his book that miners and their families occupied the dwellings while the larger buildings consisted of boarding houses, saloons, and perhaps some fandango houses. He quotes a newspaper reporter of the day who visited the suburb and described what he saw:

"The all-pervading saloon men have established themselves in the neighborhood, and no doubt a closer search would discover all the other accessories of mining camp life."[1]

Adds Wedertz:
"Miners who wished to be close to their work had begun the suburb in the earliest years of the camp. Uncle Dan Olsen (an associate of several of Bodie's earliest families—the Horners, the Butlers and the Kernohans—and who worked in Aurora and then Bodie, even before Bodie's boom years) kept a stone cabin on High Peak while mining there

in the 1860s. As the ridge above the town became dotted with hoisting works, larger mining companies erected boarding houses near their mines to keep the miners away from town and on the job. One of the most popular on the hill in 1880 was Mrs. Head's Addenda Boarding House (named after the Addenda mine). Capt. R. F. Lord, superintendent of the McClinton, had the highest residence of anyone in Bodie. It was situated near the apex of High Peak at an elevation of nearly 9,000 feet."[2]

The Bodie Standard News of December 15, 1878, quoted a Grass Valley businessman who had visited the town: "Bodie has a population of about 5,000, including the suburb on the hill."[3] A tour of this area to the east of Bodie and the historic state park property was made by the authors by authorization of the now defunct Bodie Consolidated Mining Co. which held a patent lease on 550 acres there and proposed establishment of a modern mining operation along the east side of Bodie Bluff. The company's property included the suburb area.

Clear evidence of that yesteryear life exists in the form of material remaining, such as broken crockery, metal utensils, glass, nails, stone and foundation material. Our tour guide was Mark L. Whitehead, former chief geologist for Bodie Consolidated. The area and historic remains had been left untouched by the mining firm by agreement with Mono County at the time the company was granted permission to do its core sampling.

CROCKERY FROM ENGLAND: These remains are clear evidence of life
that existed in Bodie's "suburb" up on the bluff above the town.
(A Jim Watson photo)

BIG BAD BODIE: HIGH SIERRA GHOST TOWN · 97 ·

Whitehead stated geological testing definitely proved a great deal of gold remains within Bodie Bluff and Standard Hill as well as considerable silver deposits in the Silver Hill area.

As has been mentioned in a previous chapter, the rail line extending from Mono Mills to Bodie was completed November 14, 1881, and its terminus was located directly above Bodie. The depot was constructed in the saddle of Bodie Bluff that divides Standard Hill at the north and Silver Hill at the south. The narrow gauge line was three feet in width and 32-1/2 miles long, designed to tap the forests south of Mono Lake. The railroad construction cost was $460,000. Four locomotives were hauled across the difficult terrain from the railhead at Carson City to Bodie for use on the new railroad. The locomotives were named "Tybo," "Mono," "Inyo," and "Bodie,"

The two-story depot still stands, almost out of sight from the main streets of Bodie. Billeb, who was hired by the railroad owners, Mono Lake Lumber Co., as superintendent of operations in April, 1908, 17 years after the line began service and during a period of inactivity, described his arrival in Bodie that year:

"We took the train from Tonopah to Thorne, thence by stage seven miles to Hawthorne, where we transferred to the six-horse Concord stage for the 35-mile trip across the state line to Bodie...soon I moved to the railroad office building on the hill. This was a solid two-story structure, well built on a stone foundation, substantial enough to withstand the heavy storms and high winds that often buffeted the hilltop. The main floor was mostly a large room used as the office. It had a counter running along two sides, with the high desks and stools behind it. There was a large safe with 'Bodie Bank' lettered above the doors." (This safe arrived at the depot in May, 1882 after the Bodie Bank voluntarily closed its doors and liquidated its assets as the town continued its decline. The old vault was purchased by the railroad.)

"Adjoining the main office was a smaller room with desk and office furniture; this was my private office. Behind the main office was the kitchen and a room sometimes used for boarding train crews; further back was the woodshed and beyond that the toilet, under cover. Upstairs was a large room used as a sitting room or bedroom, and four smaller bedrooms.

"Heat was supplied by wood stoves. Coal oil and gasoline lamps were used for illumination until electricity became available about 1912."

(This power was generated by the Pacific Power Co. plant at Copper Mountain—a plant rebuilt in the summer of 1911 after a disastrous avalanche destroyed the original facility in March of that year—see Chapter 10.)

"Water had to be laboriously packed in buckets from the town reservoir on the hilltop, a couple of hundred yards away from the office building. This was a particularly difficult chore during winter storms and cold. At such times we melted snow on the stoves to furnish water for washing and cleaning.

"The overflow pipe line from Rough Creek Springs, about five miles away, brought water to the reservoir, which also served in winter as a source for ice, harvested when eight or more inches thick. It was cut and stored under sawdust in ice houses and sheds to preserve it for summer use in Bodie's saloons, restaurants, hotels and stores.

"Also on the hill was the Bodie terminal's big barn. Every morning and evening the horses had to be led nearly a quarter of mile to the reservoir for water. It was a struggle to get them there in the winter, what with pushing a trail through the deep snow and breaking ice in the reservoir to get at the water."[4]

Billeb notes that the rail yard contained several sidings where cordwood, lumber and poles were stacked, in addition to a loading platform. The leveled area developed for these activities remains adjacent the old headquarters building, and the railroad right of way leading away to the south and around the hills can still be observed.

Occasionally some weathered ties can be seen along the old right-of-way near Mono Lake when the wind whisks away the cover of dirt and sand. Years of harsh weather and disuse have weighed heavily on the old two-story depot, both inside and on the exterior. Some rooms continue to carry the appearance of the "old days" of a century ago. Still covering the walls of one of the first floor rooms is wallpaper with a "various modes of travel motif" hung in 1892 and still in relatively good condition.

Near the depot is an outbuilding of unknown date, used in the 1960s by "hippies" who frequented several Bodie structures and occupied them as living quarters during the warmer summer months.

GRANITE DRILLING CONTESTS: This granite block, complete with octagonal-shaped metal hand drill, is located just over the crest of Bodie Bluff, below the old railroad depot. Holes in the block were drilled during Independence Day or Labor Day drilling contests. (A Jim Watson photo)

Located 200 feet below the depot on the hillside to the east "over on the other side from Bodie" is an almost-white granite block used in "single-jack" and "double-jack" drilling contests of skill which were an important part of Bodie's raucous Independence Day and Labor Day celebrations. The block contains holes drilled into the rock by miners who participated in those competitive fetes more than 130 years ago, and an actual octagonal-shaped metal drill remains in one of the holes in the granite. The tests of skill consisted of drilling holes which, under actual mining conditions, would then be filled with blasting powder. The contest drilling periods were timed. The miners who drilled to a measured depth within the shortest period were the winners.

The single-jack contest involved one man; the double-jack competition involved one man holding the metal drill shaft, giving it a partial turn between blows, while a second miner wielded the heavy hammer, and woe to the drill shaft holder if he who wielded the hammer had imbibed a bit too much during the celebration!

Perhaps within the near future the granite block, complete with metal drill, can be transported to Main Street by park rangers so that it can be viewed by the many thousands who visit Bodie each year. Whether a story in the June 25, 1932 Bridgeport Chronicle-Union and Bodie

Chronicle referred to this particular granite block on the hill, or another block, is not known, but this comment was made in the newspaper:

"'Bodie died in 1931' someone had written on the stone which has in the past been used for drilling contests on Main Street."[5]

These drilling contests resulted in at least one family moving to the mining town about 1931. Mrs. Alma Brunner, listed as 84 years of age when she was interviewed by a reporter in April 1989, in Douglas Flat, Calaveras County, California, told of her late husband, Melvin, winning a drilling contest that year in Bodie. As a result he was offered a job by a mining company superintendent. He took the position as a powder man, and this led a short time later to a mining accident in which he suffered a broken back.

As Mrs. Brunner put it: "Some green kid set his charges while Melvin was still lighting a fuse. It took him three years to get well even though they told him he'd never walk again. He went back to the mines, Winnemucca, Getchell, Copper Canyon, wherever there was a need for a powder man."[6]

OLD CYANIDE STORAGE TANK: The circular debris in the foreground is the remains of a cyanide tank up on Bodie Bluff that was part of the Treadwell-Yukon Company cyanide plant destroyed by a fire in 1946. The tall structure beyond is the old railroad depot and water tank to the right. (A Jim Watson photo)

Another item of historical interest on the bluff is the foundation of the cyanide plant destroyed by fire in 1946. This plant, owned by the Alaska Treadwell-Yukon Co., began operations January 10, 1931. The cyanide process removed up to 90 percent of the gold from ore. In the Bridgeport Chronicle-Union & Bodie Chronicle issue of January 10, 1931, is this story:

"TREADWELL YUKON CO. NOW OPERATING TWO MILLS: The Treadwell-Yukon Co. is now operating both of its mills at Bodie. The Standard Mill is handling between 30 and 40 tons per day of ore from the south end mines...the new mill on the hill above the Standard mill is in operation and the crushing portion is working to the best advantage for treatment of ores from the old Standard dumps."[7]

Things had changed during that year and the following February 1932, the Bridgeport Chronicle-Union and Bodie Chronicle carried a much more disheartening story based on the Treadwell-Yukon operations:

"QUITS AT BODIE—The past week saw about the last of the Treadwell-Yukon Co.'s operations at Bodie. The company during the two years of its operations at the old mining camp spent many thousands of dollars in its efforts to find ways and means for extracting the ore values from the old Standard Hill dumps, and without sufficient success to warrant, they said, further operations. Two truckloads of machinery were sent to Bridgeport and from that point to Minden for shipment by rail to other points."

The 1946 fire ended any major efforts to retrieve gold from the property.

The original Standard mill below had burned in October, 1898, but a 20-stamp mill was rebuilt immediately as a replacement and this added a resurgence to gold processing in Bodie as electricity was brought on line, but by 1909 Bodie was again in decline. Small operators mined ore occasionally between 1900 and the advent of the State Park operation in 1962. J.S. Cain aided many of these operators. He purchased the gold produced from tailings and various small diggings until the 1932 fire burned his bank. He continued, however, to believe Bodie would have a resurgence until the day he died in 1939 in San Francisco, California.

Other interesting highlights to be seen in the "Suburb" include a large depression in the earth on the hillside above the cyanide plant site. This depression was caused by the collapse of old mine tunneling in 1888 which dropped the earth from four to eight feet at the surface in a great sudden whoosh of air. Witnesses said the resulting concussion, similar to an explosion, broke windows in buildings down the hillside in Bodie.

This suburb area involved numerous attempts to mine gold up until World War II. The war ended gold mining by edict of President Franklin D. Roosevelt. In 1928, however, the Treadwell-Yukon interests had moved into Bodie and a mineshaft was driven into the hills, although it proved unsuccessful, due mainly to the advent of the Great Depression of the 1930s. The company collapsed, similarly, perhaps, with a "great whoosh" like those tunnels 30 years earlier.

The hard financial times had not discouraged another firm, calling itself "Roseklip," a composite of the names of its founders, Henry Klipstein, formerly with Anglo-American Mining, and Jack Rosekrans of the Spreckles interests. The firm obtained leases for Cain Company properties and established an open pit mining operation, employing the use of steam shovels for the first time in Bodie. This endeavor ended in failure and, in turn, was succeeded by yet another little-known mining firm known as Bodie Gilford Mining Company. It, too, was unsuccessful. At the time it halted operations due to World War II, Bodie Gilford was working a 500,000-ton waste dump.

Following the war the Standard cyanide plant was refurbished by a successor to the Bodie Gilford firm, an organization calling itself "Sierra Mines." The 1946 fire that destroyed the plant also put an end to Sierra's endeavors. The plant burned to the ground just 10 days after it opened.

Results of the Roseklip operations can be seen in tailings on Bodie Bluff. "Bites" taken out of the piles by the steam shovels are clearly evident. The cyanide plant remains nearby also are in evidence—the old foundation as well as the circular cyanide storage tank's collapsed sheet metal sides. The tank itself was partially melted by the intense heat. Also piled adjacent to the site is a gray-white powdery material called "trona"—hydrous acid sodium carbonate, a material used in the cyanide process. This system of leaching gold from ore has been basic since its discovery in Europe in 1887.

The old Standard Consolidated cyanide plant located at the north edge of Bodie also was destroyed by fire eight years later in 1954. It had remained unused from shortly after the turn of the century until 1932 when Roseklip reactivated it and operated it for nine years, until 1941. The remains of this plant no longer exist.

As for the remains of the cyanide plant facilities on the bluff, a machine shop in a wood frame structure, with some machinery still intact as well as a laboratory, still exist, weathered, but much as they existed following the 1946 fire. During the intervening years souvenir hunters and squatters have taken their toll.

The Bodie Suburb referred to by authors and scribes of earlier days, of course, no longer exists, but those items that remain on the surface draw a picture for us of the life and activities that went on there more than a century ago. Had it not been for J.S. Cain and his family, this most likely would be the situation in the Bodie townsite. The family has successfully saved most of what is seen today by hiring security personnel, and the State of California and the Friends of Bodie organization have continued to work to protect the fragile old town.

As for the "suburb," left unexplained is what happened to the 100-plus structures—the dwellings, commercial establishments, rooming houses, etc., that stood up there on the bluff during the town's peak years. Some probably burned; some might have collapsed; probably many more were dismantled as mining operations were phased out and needed building materials were hauled down the hill for use in repairing structures in town and/or for erecting a few new ones, in Bodie and elsewhere. Whatever the case, none of the suburb remains, with the exception of the old railroad depot and an old water tower. The visitor experiences an eerie feeling standing up there on the bluff with the wind whistling past his ears and realizing that here once existed a lively "Bodie Suburb."

The Bodie Evening Miner, in a July 1882 edition, carried this story, indicating the suburb still existed and was actually growing at that time, and was referred to as "Piute Flat" and "Squaw Flat":

"PIUTE FLAT—This suburb of Bodie, on the eastern side of the hill, is improving very rapidly since the opening up of the placer diggings there. Mike Wilson and Ogden are putting up new buildings there—or rather have removed old buildings to the flat, which are being fitted up as good as new. Johnny Edwards is also putting a new and improved clock on the ground. And we are told that electric lights will soon be in use at the diggings. Piute (or rather Squaw Flat) is bound to boom."[8]

No explanation was made in the story as to what the "improved clock" could be. Perhaps the suburb had an unreliable clock that was being replaced. It was interesting to note that the story indicated that to the contrary, that Mike Wilson and Ogden "have removed old buildings to the flat, which are being fitted up as good as new," indicating that rather than removing structures for use elsewhere, just the reverse was happening.

The indication was that "the suburb" was booming in 1882. [9]

FOOTNOTES — CHAPTER 9

1. Wedertz, page 16
2. Ibid, pages 37, 38
3. Bodie Standard News, December 15, 1878
4. Billeb, page 37
5. Bridgeport Chronicle-Union and Bodie Chronicle, June 25, 1932
6. Calaveras Enterprise, April 26, 1989
7. Bridgeport Chronicle-Union and Bodie Chronicle, January 10, 1931
8. Ibid, February 6, 1932
9. The Bodie Evening Miner began publication May 8, 1882, with Mr. Jones as Editor and Mr. Curry as Founder-Publisher, July 19, 1882

CHAPTER 10

THE AVALANCHES OF 1911

Three fatal avalanches in a 1911 blizzard took the lives of nine Mono County residents–seven in a single slide–in what remains a record number of Mono County deaths attributed to a single storm.

The seven-death avalanche occurred at a newly completed Pacific Power Company hydroelectric plant located at Copper Mountain, 15 miles southwest of Bodie at the west edge of the Mono Lake basin. The plant was providing most of Bodie with electricity.

The eighth victim was killed in an avalanche at the Crystal Lake Gold Mining Company at Lundy, a small mining community farther west of the Copper Mountain site. The ninth death resulted from a snowslide at a gold mine in Masonic, another tiny mining town 15 miles northwest of Bodie.

THE SWAZEY HOTEL: Looking like anything but a hotel, this wood structure has the help of a prop to keep it from falling over from old age. The support is an example of the State of California's policy of "arrested decay." It's tough to survive a Bodie winter. (A Jim Watson photo)

That winter of 1910-11 was not especially harsh by high country standards. A "normal" winter in Bodie could often equal the worst winter elsewhere. The 8,396-foot altitude is more than a mile-and-a-half up. Temperatures drop to 40 degrees below zero, and occasionally more. Blizzards can last for days. In fact, that's just what this one did in 1911. March had come in like a lion.

Accompanying high winds buffeted the mountains and canyons surrounding Bodie beginning March 6 and continued without let-up for 36 hours. Deep drifts built up along canyon walls and on mountainsides throughout the Mono County area.

The pack deepened on the slopes of Copper Mountain while 1,500 feet below lay the hydroelectric plant that had begun operation in the final days of December, 1910. Asleep in two concrete cottages and two cabins near the power facility were eight people. As the new generators hummed, electricity was lighting the lamps and electric heaters recently purchased by residents and businesses in Bodie and five Nevada communities further east—Aurora, Lucky Boy, Hawthorne, Fairview and Wonder.

LIKE TWO SOLDIERS AT ATTENTION: These two old Shell gasoline
pumps stand on Bodie's Main Street through foul weather and fair, ready
to dispense petrol to vehicles in need. But alas, they serve fuel no more and
are but staunch landmarks in the historic State Park. (A Jim Watson photo)

Suddenly, between midnight and 2 a.m. that fateful March 7, 1911, the tremendous weight of snow on the mountainside gave way and with a roar bore down on the unsuspecting occupants of the dwellings, asleep in their warm beds. Within seconds the powerhouse and cottages were ripped off their foundations and flattened. Wiped away, too, without trace in the great sheet of white was an abandoned smelter nearby which had stood on that spot for more than 30 years.

Seven of the eight died where they slept. Their deaths listed in the Mono County coroner's log in the courthouse in Bridgeport, the county seat, are:

CRUDE HEADSTONE: This is one of seven concrete markers apparently
fashioned from portions of concrete slabs that comprised the walls of
Copper Mountain Power House cottages. The victim, J. Javeaux, had his
initials "J J" reversed. (A Jim Watson photo)

AVALANCHE VICTIM: Although there was a question about his identity and the spelling of his name at the time of his death, the headstone of
this 1911 Jordan avalanche victim is listed on the concrete marker as "B.
PESEN, DIED MARCH 7, 1911." This is a misspelling for the name
"PESSEN'. (A Jim Watson photo)

HARRY W. WEIR: Although officially referred to as "Harry W. Weir,"
this victim of the avalanche has a headstone that identifies him as "H.M.
Wier": wrong spelling, wrong initials. (A Jim Watson photo)

NOT A JORDAN VICTIM: Also buried with the seven who died in the
Jordan Avalanche is "DEL ORME KNOWLTON JR.," killed March 7,
1911, the same day as the others, but who was crushed in a similar avalanche that destroyed a small power plant in Lundy, five miles away. His
headstone carries the name "D.O. KNOWLTON." (A Jim Watson photo)

PATRICK STROMBLAD IS BURIED HERE: Killed in the 1911
Avalanche with six others, his headstone is the only one showing care.
Someone has erected a wrought iron fence around his grave and replaced
the crude original marker with this white headstone. The name
"Stromblad" is misspelled "STORMBLAD." (A Jim Watson photo)

NOT DEAD ACCORDING TO CORONER: Samuel M. Smith died in
his Masonic mine from an avalanche March 7 or 8, 1911 and is buried in
Bridgeport Cemetery. This is his headstone. No record of his death exists
in the Mono County Courthouse. (A Jim Watson photo)

John Javernaux, about 40, single, a laborer
Patrick Stromblad, about 40, single, a laborer
P.N. Peacock, about 45, single, a plant operator
Robert H. Mason, 32, married, chief plant operator
Harry W. Weir, about 20, single, a laborer
Roland Harden, 25, single, a laborer
Ben Pessen, 22, single, a laborer. [1]

A few days after the Copper Mountain tragedy the victim of the Lundy slide that occurred just five miles away was identified as Del Orme Knowlton Jr., 29, an electrician. He had been in charge of the plant and was on watch at 10 p.m. that Tuesday night, March 6, when that avalanche occurred. His body was found in the powerhouse ruins, seated against the generator. The ninth avalanche victim, in Masonic, was Samuel M. Smith, 50, a gold mine operator.

The coroner lists the cause of deaths from the Copper Mountain slide as: "Death by an avalanche of snow while on duty in the employ of the Pacific Power Co. at their plant at Copper Mountain," and the place of burial as "Jordan." [2]

This was a tiny community near the Copper Mountain power plant. The town has long since faded into oblivion.

The power plant cottages had contained eight persons and just seven were killed. But what of victim number eight? By some miracle Mrs. Agnes Mason, the wife of the chief plant operator, survived the holocaust. The story of her ordeal will be told shortly. Concentration will remain on the seven killed and of the confusion and inaccurate reports involving their identities discovered in research by the authors.

As noted, the Copper Mountain seven were listed by the coroner, in this case A.G. Allen, Mono County "ex-officio coroner," as all being employees for the power company. This differs from a news story in the March 11 edition of the Bridgeport Chronicle-Union and Bodie Chronicle (a combined publication). The newspaper stated four of the seven killed were miners who were spending the winter in company-owned cottages at the powerhouse site. Two names in the story also were different: Stromblad and Pessen were the same, but the newspaper listed the remaining two as "Harold Hardy" and "John Sullivan." [3]

The authors, in researching materials involving the avalanches, determined that the "John Sullivan" listed by the newspaper as a victim was apparently the "John Javernaux" as identified in the coroner's records. A newspaper reporter in a hurry could easily have mistaken a handwritten name in a legal document.

The authors also determined that ironically, whether the name was "Sullivan" or "Javerneaux"—the body was buried with the other victims in a small gravesite in the old townsite of Jordan, but not beneath a gravestone bearing either name. No, the stone bears the name "J. Javeaux" and the date of the avalanche, "March 7, 1911" as do the other avalanche victims' headstones. Both the "J" letters in the Javeaux marker are written in reverse. And, to further complicate the identities, the name "J. Javeaux" does not appear as the name of an avalanche victim in any newspaper story of the day, nor does the name "John Javernaux." Neither does the name "J. Javeaux" appear in the coroner's records as a slide victim. And the authors found no evidence of a "Sullivan" nor a "Javernaux" being buried at the mass gravesite at Jordan.

Strangely, too, there is no evidence that "P.N. Peacock," listed by the coroner as an avalanche victim, is interred in the mass burial site. The coroner does state, however, in his courthouse records, that Peacock is buried at that site. The authors found no headstone bearing his name, although it appears a grave might be located in a space between the headstones of Harry W. Weir and Patrick Stromblad. Someone might have removed or stolen the Peacock headstone.

With these inconsistencies in mind, let's return to that avalanche and listen to Emil W. Billeb, that Bodie Railroad official, describe the situation of early March, 1911. The storm had begun March 6 and during the following night he recalls that electric service in Bodie suddenly went dead, pitching the town into an eerie blackness and forcing residents to get out their oil lamps for illumination.

Billeb joined the rescue party formed to travel to the powerhouse after word was received the blackout was due not to downed power lines but rather to a powerhouse disaster. Here is his description of the scene:

"The storm let up the next day and efforts began on the monumental task of digging out and opening roads about town and to the outside world...telephone communication was also disrupted by the storm and it was not until the next morning we had our first word from outside. It came by way of Mono Mills where the caretaker had been trying for 17 hours to make a connection with Bodie."[4]

The power plant had been built at the site of that earlier-day smelter. Water from Mill Creek dropped through the penstocks to the powerhouse and the site had been considered safe, having never suffered a slide or an avalanche that anyone could remember—until that fateful night of March 7, 1911.

The facility stood "at least 1,000 feet from the base of Copper Mountain," the Bridgeport Chronicle Union and Bodie Chronicle reported. "It was built of reenforced concrete and within a few hundred feet were two concrete cottages for the use of employees and their families." The story states the Masons occupied one cottage while a second was occupied by Peacock and his assistant, Weir, an electrician and lineman. "Within a short distance was a cabin occupied by John Sullivan, Harold Hardy, Ben Pessner, miners."[5]

The authors believe that "Harold Hardy" mentioned probably is Roland Harden and "Pessner" is Ben Pessen. No "Harold Hardy" is listed as a casualty by the coroner, whereas he does list Roland Harden.

The newspaper story goes on to say: "At the old smelter, some 600 to 700 feet from the powerhouse and up another hill lived Patrick Stromblad, a miner. The four miners were spending the winter in these old buildings and were not employed by the power company. Between midnight and 2 o'clock in the morning the slide came, destroyed the plant, cottages, smelter and other buildings. All the bodies have been recovered. Coffins were taken from Bodie and on Thursday (March 16, 1911) the unfortunates were given interment at Jordan."

As we know, the Copper Mountain plant was not the first to supply Bodie with electricity. The hydroelectric facility just a few miles north on Green Creek and west of present Highway 395 had been producing power for machinery at the Standard Mill and several other milling facilities plus a few businesses in Bodie since October, 1893, a period of 18 years.

The Green Creek plant actually holds a unique place in history, as, in this instance, does Bodie. Until the Green Creek powerplant had begun generation of electricity that day in 1893, power had never been delivered by wire from the source of generation to the point of use! Green Creek was the world's first powerplant to do so—and Bodie was the world's first recipient of electricity by wire!

Delivery of power by wire had been thought to be impossible until James Stuart Cain, chief stockholder of Bodie's Standard Consolidated Mining Company and several other properties in Bodie, determined in that year of 1893 that it could be done. Besides that, he needed electricity to power mills and pumps at Bodie. Burning prodigious amounts of wood that had to be hauled by rail from Mono Mills to produce steam had proven too expensive.

With the aid of Thomas H. Legget, superintendent of the Standard Consolidated Mine, Cain prevailed in stringing the power line. Skeptics had not only believed it was impossible to transmit electricity by wire, they also determined in their own minds that if it was tried, the electricity would jump off into space at the first turn in the line. Cain laughed at this idea, but he did condescend to have the power line run in a straight line over the mountains from Green Creek to Bodie. And the wire he used was square in shape, as were the nails used in those days.[6]

After Green Creek proved a success, Cain continued to assist in financing other Eastern Sierra Nevada hydroelectric plants, including the ill-fated Copper Mountain facility. Legget, too, went on to bigger and better things. He was hired by the British Government to assist in building power plants from Rhodesia to Australia.

Cain's daughter-in-law, Ella M. Cain, authored a book, "The Story of Bodie," in which she wrote about her father-in-law:

"After Green Creek plant was built, Jim Cain located other power sites in Mono County…he realized here was potential power for the cities of the south, and, sooner or later, they would need them. Holding these power sites was a big expense, as the law required that work developing them had to be done continuously. When ranches controlling water rights were for sale, Jim bought them. He finally received a worthwhile offer for his holdings from the Pacific Power Co., receiving, as part consideration, a large block of stock in the new company."[7]

Returning to the 1911 avalanches, it was obvious to Billeb that Jim Cain would want to know about the situation, but it was some time before he could be informed. It took Jack Hammond, a Bodie area resident who owned Hammond's Station and organizer of the search team, the entire night to reach the operator at Bodie and until 8 a.m. the day after the storm let up to finally inform Cain. Hammond organized a search party but visibility was poor due to a heavy freezing fog, described by the Indians as "pokonip." With Bodie's physician, Dr. O.F. Krebs, the rescue party headed for the powerhouse site. Travel was difficult on skis. They were equipped with a single toe strap that bound them to the boot and a cleat that fit against the heel.

Even when rescuers arrived at the avalanche scene after traveling many hours, it took many more hours to find the flattened powerhouse which was covered with 10 to 20 feet of snow. No buildings were visible. Searchers probed with rods while others shoveled trenches. Above the plant site evidence of the slide was apparent on the steep mountain slope but the "pokonip" made it difficult to determine the full extent of the damage.

While rescuers probed for survivors, seventy men and 10 horses were thrashing about in an attempt to clear the road from Bodie to the plant site. Drifts were up to ten feet deep. After one entire day only two miles had been cleared. By noon the second day a mile and a half had been added when another blizzard blew in. The snow froze to the faces of the men; horses had difficulty remaining upright and rescuers began suffering snow blindness and frostbite. Efforts finally were halted when it was determined it would take a week to clear the road. It was at about this time that Lundy and Masonic were crushed by avalanches.

The rescue team at the hydroelectric plant began finding bodies beneath the flattened concrete cottages. After several more hours of probing and digging a scream was heard from deep beneath the snow. The searchers renewed their efforts and after digging down eight feet, discovered Mrs. Mason alive. She was pinned in bed beside the body of her husband who had been crushed. The Mason's cottage was flattened but as luck would have it one of the concrete wall slabs had caught on an iron bedpost. This provided a partial roof to protect Mrs. Mason from the weight of the snow and broken walls.

The Mason's dog had been sleeping on their bed and the heat of the animal's body helped both her and the dog survive for the 2-1/2 days they were buried. A final survivor was a cat uncovered as rescuers shoveled away the snow. It jumped up out onto the snow, took one look at the rescue party and promptly ran away.

Mrs. Mason was placed on a sled fashioned of sheet iron by the rescue team. She was transported by sleigh to the Hammond Ranch where she was treated for hypothermia and shock as well as an injured leg. At that point she was placed on a toboggan and pulled across the snow 16 miles to Bodie where she remained for a week; pulled on another sleigh 10 miles to a road and placed in an automobile; driven to Thorne, Nevada, the nearest rail connection; placed on a train and transported to Oakland; removed to an ambulance and finally admitted to Fabiola

Hospital where physicians determined her right leg had become infected. They amputated at the knee.

Mrs. Mason later returned to Bodie and herself became an employee of the Pacific Power Company for whom her late husband had worked. She remained there for many years. This was most likely a decision made by Jim Cain who, by then, was a major stockholder in the company.[8]

A visit to Jordan and the gravesite of the avalanche victims leaves one with a feeling of quiet serenity and loneliness. The graves are grouped together on a small bluff overlooking the Mono Lake Basin about a mile north of the old powerhouse site. Copper Mountain looks down from above and a penstock extends out over a steep precipice. At the base a small Southern California Edison Co. powerplant hums about a quarter-mile from the original site, delivering its electricity over lines supported by wood poles to customers throughout the eastern California and western Nevada area.

It is known that buried within the small Jordan enclosure are six of the seven slide victims and perhaps the seventh, Peacock. Surprisingly there is one additional headstone, that of Knowlton, who was killed in Lundy. The Bridgeport newspaper of March 18 stated that Knowlton's remains might possibly be sent east for interment in New York State where his relatives resided, but obviously this did not happen and he rests forever in that lonely little plot with his fellow avalanche victims.[9]

All of the headstones are small and appear to have been prepared by an amateur stonemason. They also appear to have been fashioned from portions of concrete slabs that comprised the walls of the powerhouse cottages. The gravesite itself is enclosed by a wire cyclone-type fence with a gate and is kept clean and clear of brush and debris. Only Stromblad's grave indicates special care. Someone in the past has erected a wrought iron picket fence around it within the mass gravesite and has replaced the crude original marker with a modern marble headstone, but with the name misspelled "Stromblad." The original marker remains, however, leaning near the newer headstone.

An original three-strand wire fence with wood posts once enclosed the entire 12 by 40-foot gravesite. The weathered posts, some still with square nails embedded, are scattered in the sagebrush surrounding the site, apparently lying where they were discarded when the newer fence was erected. A search by the authors of the area surrounding the gravesite failed to disclose any sign of a missing Peacock headstone. It is possible that he was not buried here.

Mrs. Anna Alena DeChambeau McKenzie, in our 1989 interview, recalled the Copper Mountain Avalanche. She was 12 years of age and said she remembered that the body of one of the victims was shipped to San Francisco by his family for burial, but she was unable to recall who it was.

On the other hand, Billeb wrote that the seven who died in the slide were buried at Jordan. He did not list their names but indicated they were the Copper Mountain victims. He did not mention the other fatal avalanches that occurred that March. The Bridgeport newspaper of March 18, 1911, stated all bodies were recovered. "Coffins were taken from Bodie and on Thursday (March 16) the unfortunates were given interment at Jordan."[10]

Mention has been made of the slide in Masonic and the victim, Samuel M. Smith. By some strange quirk, the Mono County coroner's records do not list his death but newspapers carried the story of his demise in an avalanche, stating he had been married and was divorced two years prior to his death. His former wife and two children resided in Santa Rosa at the time and the news stories indicated he was well known in Bridgeport. He was buried in the Bridgeport Cemetery beside a brother who had died three years previously. The authors found both Smiths' headstones in the cemetery.

The "1911 Avalanches of Mono County" have been reviewed for the first time. We know how many perished—nine. We know the places of burial—Jordan and Bridgeport with Peacock's interment site still a mystery. Whether there actually existed a John Sullivan or a John Javernaux—probably they and J. Javeaux are the same. Whether Harold Hardy actually was Roland Harden, most likely. And whether Annie McKenzie was correct in her recollection about one victim's remains being sent to another location—just not known and she could not remember.

Whatever the circumstances, the Jordan gravesite is certainly a part of Bodie's history. It is just off a private gravel road west of Highway 395, three-fourths of a mile north of the road to Lundy in the Mono Lake Basin. The road curves northerly toward a row of small trees. The gravesite is visible to the east of the trees and located in the same bluff are the remains of a stone foundation of a small structure, perhaps an old Jordan dwelling.

What of the Copper Mountain hydroelectric plant following the avalanche? It was rebuilt in a more protected location near the same site and, as mentioned, resumed operation in June, 1911. The Pacific Power Company was later sold to the California Electric Company which became Pacific Electric Power Company and eventually today's Southern California Edison Company.

The site of the demolished powerhouse is marked by a concrete foundation and several sections of steel penstock pipe still to be seen today. Several of the sections are riveted and these remnants remain above ground. Sections of penstock that delivered water down the mountainside into the powerhouse remain buried, but the tops of a portion of the lines also are exposed and can be observed at the site.

It might be noted here that author Emil Billeb, the rescue party member, and Jessie Delilah (Dolly) Cain, one of four daughters of Bodie pioneer James Stuart Cain, were married October 7, 1911, in San Francisco, exactly seven months after the "1911 Avalanches of Mono County," culminating a courtship of two years. They began married life together in a home in Bodie.

Mrs. Mason's Story

Mrs. R. H. Mason, the wife of the Copper Mountain chief plant operator killed in the March 7, 1911 avalanche, wrote a letter of thanks to her rescuers the following month while recovering from the amputation of her right leg. The letter was printed in the April 20, 1911 edition of Bridgeport Chronicle-Union and Bodie Chronicle, headed: "MRS. R.H. MASON IS VERY GRATEFUL.[11]

"Mrs. R. H. Mason, who had the terrible experience at Copper Mountain last month, and who is now in the Fabiola Hospital at Oakland has sent the following for publication:

"On the night of March 7th a severe snowslide came down Copper Mountain at Jordan and carried away the power plant and all the buildings of the Pacific Power Company, also a cabin and an older smelter which had been there thirty years. All the people in camp, eight in number, were buried. After 60 hours Mrs. R. H. Mason and her dog were found alive. Mr. Mason who was beside her in bed was killed, as were the six other men. The concrete cottage of the Mason's was crushed and the head of their bed was bent over them. A slab of concrete caught on a chair and trunk, held there by a margin of an inch and a half, and that saved

Mrs. Mason and the dog. She was wedged in and could not move. She dreamed she was rescued and in Bodie and thought another slide caught her again.

"It took the rescuers three hours to dig and saw her out of the hole and Mrs. Mason directed them as to the best way of doing it and has at all times been perfectly conscious. She was under eight feet of snow. When found she told them she knew she had been there three days and nights and the second day heard them walking over her. She screamed and the dog barked but they did not hear her. They found the tracks where they had walked, as she had said.

"The men who worked so hard in the rescue of the bodies and getting Mrs. Mason out were L.A. Larson who found her, P.G. Sexton, Paul Greenleaf, George Denham, Ernest Valverde, Herb DeChambeau, J.E. Wagner and Eddie LaVette. They made a sled of sheet iron and pulled her, the men on skis, to John Conway's Ranch, where every attention was given her for her comfort and welfare. Strange to say, no bones were broken, but she is suffering from a bad knee where it touched her husband's body. Her hair did not turn white as was reported.

"Eighty men worked for days to get the road broken from Bodie to Jordan, so they could take her to Bodie. Mrs. Mason is very grateful to the men who rescued her and the snowshoe team, consisting of Ed Cody, Andrew and John Sturgeon, Denny Thompson, Arthur Murphy, Ernest Valverde and P.G. Sexton. These were joined by Mr. Greenleaf, Jimmie Cain and Earl Bell, the latter part of the journey. She also wishes to thank all others who have shown their kindness to her.

"I also want to thank Mrs. P.G. Sexton, who has taken such good care of me and been so very kind during my sickness and trouble. Also the four young men who walked to Del Monte, taking me on a sleigh—George Denham, Mr. Billeb, Stuart Denham, and Denny Thompson. The people of Bodie have been very fine and have been so good to me that I can never begin to thank them for all their kindness to me—J.S. Cain and family, Mrs. A.F. Dieter, Mrs. Arthur Reading, Mr. Murphy, George Denham and all of my many friends I wish thanked through your paper. (signed) Mrs. R. H. Mason, Fabiola Hospital, Oakland, CA."[11]

FOOTNOTES — CHAPTER 10

1. Mono County Courthouse records, Bridgeport, California
2. Ibid
3. Bridgeport Chronicle-Union and Bodie Chronicle, March 11, 1911
4. Billeb, page 158
5. Bridgeport Chronicle-Union and Bodie Chronicle, March 11, 1911
6. Barbara Moore, "Bodie Electrifies the World," page 7, The Album, Times and Tales of Inyo-Mono, Vol I, No. 3, July 1988
7. Ella Cain, "The Story of Bodie," page 85
8. Billeb, page 160 Bridgeport Chronicle-Union and Bodie Chronicle, March 18, 1911
10. Ibid
11. Ibid, April 20, 1911

CHAPTER 11

AURORA—THE MARK TWAIN INVOLVEMENT

Tales of Bodie must include mention of Aurora, often considered Bodie's "Sister City" of the high Sierra, and, of course, Aurora's most famous citizen, Mark Twain.

MARK TWAIN MAY HAVE VISITED BODIE: Although Bodie, during the 1860s, was not yet a developed town, it was near Aurora and might have been visited by Twain during his tenure as a freelance writer. It was in Aurora that Twain and his friend, Calvin Higbie, considered themselves "millionaires for ten days" after acquiring the Wide West Gold Mine in Esmeralda, only to lose it through unusual circumstances. (Photo from a private collection)

Aurora is located at 7,500 feet in Nevada, eight miles east of Bodie. A vehicle trip from Bodie to the old townsite, however, involves a distance of about 16 miles eastward through Bodie Canyon on rugged road recommended only for four-wheel drive vehicles. This road was even posted as "impassible" at its eastern terminus when the authors traveled it. And it was determined that the Aurora of yesterday is just that—a town of the past consisting of a cemetery fast disappearing as vandals make off with wrought iron fencing and ancient headstones they consider "souvenirs."

PAGE FROM 1864 AURORA NEWSPAPER: This is a typical front page of the "Esmeralda Daily Union" printed in Aurora, Esmeralda County, Nevada Territory, in June, 1864. The Marden & Folger's coffee advertisement notes the name "Folger," which continues to produce coffee today in San Francisco. The "MINING ROPE" ad lists the manufacturer as A.S. Hallidie & Co., which produced cable for the Standard Mine in Bodie later, and made the cable for the first cable cars in San Francisco.

The mountains surrounding Aurora are considerably higher than the townsite itself.

Adjacent to the remnants of the old mining town, when observed by the authors, was a gigantic open pit gold mine in which an entire mountain is being removed, reduced to powder, and "heap-leached" with cyanide in huge earthen vats lined with heavy sheets of plastic—one of today's modern methods of mining gold. This huge pit serves as a reminder that those miners of the past did a good job but left a lot of the precious metal. Modern mining methods are doing a more thorough job of claiming gold and silver.

There was a time when Aurora was a boom town, originally called "Esmeralda," and populated by as many as 5,000 persons, among whom was Samuel Clemens known as author Mark Twain.

Aurora's short history began in 1860 after three prospectors, J.M. Corey, E.R. Hicks and James N. Braley, found a ledge of quartz containing a heavy concentration of silver, interspersed with some gold. This was nineteen years before Bodie's peak boom period of 1879. The trio liked the word "esmeralda," Spanish for "emerald," and so was established the Esmeralda Mining District and the town of Esmeralda. The "emerald" lasted only a few short months before the name "Aurora" was determined to be more appropriate, named after the Roman goddess of dawn.

Within two years the town was thriving and Mark Twain was a prospector among the pioneers. He wrote numerous articles for the Esmeralda Star, one of two local newspapers. He also served as a correspondent for a famous Virginia City newspaper called The Territorial Enterprise and his articles based on Aurora and other mining camps of the West were later compiled by Twain as part of his book, "Roughing It."

In the first year after its founding Aurora was in a unique quandary. Its citizens believed they lived in the State of California and so petitioned the California legislature to request formation of a county which they wanted named "Mono," with Aurora to be the county seat. The legislature agreed. The Senate favored "Esmeralda" as the county's name, and the Assembly liked "Mono." The Assembly prevailed and Mono County was established with Aurora as the county seat. At almost the same time President James Buchanan authorized establishment of the Territory of Nevada, an area carved from the original Utah Territory. The new legislature of this new territory, seeing millions in gold and silver pouring out of Aurora in Mono County, California, (total bullion production was estimated at $16 million, surpassed eventually in value only by the Comstock Lode and Bodie) promptly formed a county of its own, named it "Esmeralda," determined that Aurora was actually in Nevada Territory, and selected the town as the Esmeralda County seat. The territorial legislature had unilaterally determined the town was in Nevada Territory without legal authority.

The Civil War had begun by this time and Union sympathizers had differences of opinion with those favoring the Confederacy. Fights occurred in Aurora involving fists and knives, occasionally punctuated by a shooting. Tempers flared but no one was killed. Production of precious metals was vitally needed by the Union to pay for the war.

The need for a definite boundary line and a determination of whether Aurora was in Nevada Territory or the State of California was a necessity. The governing bodies of the state and the territory agreed to a survey. This was begun, starting at Lake Tahoe, but before it could be completed election time had arrived September 2, 1863. To prevent further friction, both agencies approved dual balloting in which two slates of candidates would be voted upon, one in California and the other in Nevada Territory.

Voters for the Nevada candidates cast their ballots in the militia armory. Those voting for California candidates did so in the city jail. Everyone had the opportunity to vote twice. The Republican candidates swept both ballots. The boundary survey team a short while later determined that Aurora was in Nevada Territory by a distance of 3-1/2 miles, but the decision also left Mono County without a county seat. So, another election was held in Mono County, California and voters favored Bridgeport as their county governmental center. To settle the question as to the future of Mono County's records which were still over in Aurora, Nevada Territory, a group of Mono County residents banded together and headed for Aurora's big brick courthouse. During the raid the records were confiscated, loaded onto a wagon and transported to Bridgeport. Those who participated reported just a single casualty during the wild ride back home; one of the group toppled off the wagon landing on his head, but he was not seriously hurt. Those who observed the mishap described him as "slightly inebriated."[1]

With the border officially determined, Aurora definitely was established as Esmeralda County seat in Nevada Territory, but its days were numbered when the shallow-depth mines soon petered out and the town rapidly became a ghost town. Within a few years Goldfield was selected to replace Aurora as county seat and Aurora was included in an expanded Mineral County, with the Mineral County seat not in Aurora, but 27 miles eastward in Hawthorne, Nevada.

Aurora mining had hit its boom period rapidly and its decline just as fast. The town faded in 1865 as miners headed for Virginia City, Nevada and the Comstock Lode. As people moved away, abandoned wood structures were dismantled and the valuable building material hauled away to be used again, or the wood was burned for heat. When Bodie began its boom period 14 years later in 1879 many of the remaining structures and materials were hauled there, including a few of the numerous brick buildings that had made Aurora unusual in the days of basically all-wood construction. Wood was scarce and expensive.

During Aurora's development, brick manufacturers had seen a bright future and four brickyards provided new red bricks for construction. One, two and even three-story brick buildings were erected. Some of Aurora's brick structures were still standing as late as 1947 and W.A. Chalfant of Bishop wrote that year: "…elsewhere, brick buildings of two stories, and at least one of three stories, are open to the elements, and upon them the seal of dissolution has been set." Brick structures remaining in Aurora were sold to Southern California developers for use in fireplaces and homes.

MARK TWAIN, WIFE AND TWO OF THREE DAUGHTERS—A rare photo of Twain, wife and daughters. His family, including a son, preceded him in death and all are buried in Elmira, New York. In the 1860's, Twain lived in Esmeralda, later renamed Aurora, in Nevada, across the border from Bodie. Twain was a reporter for the Esmeralda Star and later the Virginia City, Nevada Territorial Enterprise.
(Photo from a private collection)

Mentioned earlier was Mark Twain, a young man from Hannibal, Missouri, in the mining town of Aurora, high in the Sierra Nevada Mountains. He had found his way there after his older brother, Orion Clemens, was appointed Secretary of the new Nevada Territory. In July of 1861, Orion, accompanied by Samuel, headed west from Missouri, first by steamboat, then by Overland Mail coach to Carson City, capitol of the new territory where Orion assumed his duties.

Twain could have stayed in Carson City with his brother but chose instead to seek his fortune as a prospector and speculator, occasionally returning to Carson City when his funds ran out. In September, 1862, he was hired by The Territorial Enterprise on the basis of his occasional submission of anecdotes about life in the mining camps.

Twain's career as prospector/speculator/author may have taken him during this period to the Bodie of the 1860s, but Bodie at that time was of little consequence and apparently nowhere is it noted that Twain was involved in Bodie activities.

The Mammoth City Times several years after Twain had left the area printed an excerpt it received from Chicago typifying the author's ongoing wit and wisdom:

"At the (Ulysses S.) Grant banquet in Chicago Friday night Sam Clemens responded to the last toast, 'The Babies,' as follows: 'As long as you are in your right mind never pray for twins. Twins amount to permanent riot, and there ain't any real difference between triplets and an insurrection,' which called forth shouts of laughter."[2]

Twain included experiences during his early endeavors when he compiled his book, "Roughing It"[3] and was correspondent for the Enterprise in Aurora when offered the job as city editor. He accepted and moved to Virginia City, staying with the newspaper until May, 1864, about a year. History, thereafter, records his future as an author.

Fate plays strange tricks. There was a time while Twain was in Aurora during his prospecting period in 1862, that he and a partner, Calvin Higbie, considered themselves millionaires after discovering a "blind lead," a fantastic find of gold-bearing ore in the area of a mine called the "Wide West." The laws of the district determined that to establish their claim, they must do a "fair and reasonable" amount of work on the property within ten days after the date of location or forfeit the property to public domain.

Twain no sooner found out about the requirement than a friend informed him that a close acquaintance was ill. Twain traveled to a ranch house nine miles distant to assist in nursing the ailing friend, but before leaving, left a note informing Higbie of his trip and reminding him of the work that was required at the mining claim within the ten days. They both were fully aware that there were numerous other miners eager to take over the claim if the work was not done.

Twain arrived back at the cabin on the tenth day to find Higbie sitting at a table looking forlorn with Twain's note in his hands. It seems that he, too, had gone on an important errand just after Twain had departed and had thrown a note similar to Twain's, through a broken window of the cabin since he was on horseback and in a hurry, expecting his partner to see it. This was his first opportunity to see Twain's note since he, too, had just returned and both men learned that the work required of them to keep their claim had not been done. They were still paupers.

Writes Twain in "Roughing It:" "It reads like a wild fancy sketch, but the evidence of many witnesses, and likewise that of the official records of Esmeralda District, is easily obtainable in proof that it is a true history. I can always have it to say that I was absolutely and unquestionably worth a million dollars once, for ten days."[4]

However, in the August, 1944 issue of The Pony Express, Editor Herb S. Hamlin was skeptical of Twain's claim. Hamlin wrote: "Years later, telling the story in Roughing It (which he dedicated to his Aurora partner, Calvin Higbie) Twain says he lost a million dollars when he lost the Wide West mine. This is an exaggeration. The mine never produced as much for the claim jumpers as they spent on it. Still, this much is certain; had Twain retained the Wide West, he would not have gone to Virginia City, where the foundations of his writing career were laid, and the literary history of America would be much different than it is."[5]

Hamlin is contradicted as to the eventual success of the claim by McGrath in "Gunfighters Highwaymen and Vigilantes." McGrath states: "Much to the chagrin of Higbie and Clemens, the Johnson (the name of the claim on the Wide West) became a real bonanza, producing millions of dollars worth of gold and silver."[6]

Today's visitor to Bodie Historic State Park need only look down at his feet upon visiting the Bodie Museum, which served many years as the Miners Union Hall, to be reminded of Mark Twain. For there, in the dirt street, just beyond the museum's wooden sidewalk, lies the capstone of that Aurora gold mine made famous by Twain in "Roughing It." Chiseled into the granite are the words, "Wide West." This granite piece graced the mine's overhead where Twain maintained he was made "absolutely and unquestionably worth a million dollars once, for ten days."

The stone lies just feet from the front door of the museum, and how and when it got there is a mystery.

CHISELED IN GRANITE: "WIDE WEST"—The Bodie visitor can
observe a reminder of Mark Twain, when he was a resident of nearby
Aurora in the 1860's, by looking down at the piece of granite embedded in
the dirt street in front of the Bodie Museum. There, the words "Wide
West" are chiseled in the capstone that once graced the overhead of the
mine Twain owned for ten days. (A Jim Watson photo)

FOOTNOTES — CHAPTER 11

1. Kent DeChambeau, an interview
2. Mammoth City Times, November 19, 1879
3. Mark Twain, "Roughing It," pages 254, 264
4. Ibid, page 264
5. Herb S. Hamlin, Pony Express, August, 1944
6. McGrath, page 5

CHAPTER 12

BAD, BAD, BODIE!

If ever a town deserved the nickname, "Wickedest town in the West," it was Bodie, California, during its boom period 1879 and the early 1880s. Gamblers, highwaymen, cutthroats, opium smokers, inebriates, prostitutes... if there was a name or a description of someone who operated outside the law, it would fit the riffraff of Bodie.

Other boom towns of the Old West certainly had their community lowlife, but somehow, Bodie had more than its share. Stories abound about the "Bad Man From Bodie"—a character, perhaps real but most likely fictional—who brought questionable fame to the town. The "Bad Man" was, of course, all those bad men—in Bodie and from Bodie—who lived by reputations derived from the pens of journalists who delighted in "describing" the almost daily shooting episodes that occurred in and around Bodie's many saloons.

On one occasion a total of 18 pistol shots reportedly were fired in Phillip & Moore's saloon during a cold January night in 1879. One ruffian suffered a minor head wound; a customer puffing on a smelly cigar lost the greater portion of same as the result of an errant bullet and was provided a replacement by the bartender. And, at about the same time, a barrel of ale was provided a new spout when another bullet penetrated one end of the wooden container. The Bad Man was at it again. Pat Shea and John Sloan blasted away at each other on a dance floor during a masquerade ball. Bystanders that time counted 10 bullets fired. Neither of these "crack shots" suffered a wound, and, luckily, neither did any of those counting the rounds.

There is a long list of "Bad Men" as outlined by newspaper stories. The publishers never tired of recording their exploits and the list included names such as Red Rowe, Rattlesnake Dick, James Blair, George Center, Ed Ryan, Dave Bannon, Frank Jones, John Enright, the "Mendocino Outlaw," Harry Dugan and Billy Deegan, William Baker, Henry Heif and on and on.

SAM LEON'S BAR AND THE BARBER SHOP: Once known as "The
Bodie Night Club," this bar was one of the last businesses to operate in
Bodie. Sam Leon, a Chinese, was also one of the final permanent residents.
The barber shop (right) also is the background for another photo in this
book for the Bodie Baseball Team. (A Jim Watson photo)

The pen of newspaper writer E.H. Clough was responsible for prolif-
erating the "Bad Man From Bodie" saga on the pages of the Sacramento
Bee, in Sacramento, California. His first story, 'The Bad Man of Bodie,'
appeared June 1, 1878 featuring a character called Washoe Pete.[1]

" 'I'm bad,' cried Pete in the Cosmopolitan saloon. 'I'm chief in this
yer camp, and I ken lick the man that says I ain't. I'm a raging lion on the
plains, an' every time I hit I kill. I've got an arm like a quartz stamp, an'
crush when I go fur a man. I weigh a ton an' earthquakes ain't nowhere
when I drop'."

Clough epitomized the "Bad Man From Bodie" in the following dia-
logue as printed in the October 16, 1880 issue of the Sacramento Bee:

"One of the peculiarities of a Bad Man from Bodie is his profanity. A
'Bad Man from Bodie' who never uses an oath, is as impossible as per-
petual motion or an honest election in Nevada. This trait is especially
noticeable whenever he kills a man or endeavors to kill one. Whenever
you hear of a man from Bodie who did not swear when he pulled his gun,
you may depend upon it that he is base metal, tenderfoot, a man from
Pioche, or Cheyenne, or Leadville. The oath of the 'Bad Man from Bodie'
is like the cheerful warning of the rattlesnake and, like that warning, the
blow follows close upon its heels. Whenever a 'Bad Man from Bodie'

dons his war paint and strikes the bloody trail of carnage, he is prepared
for every contingency. His little gun nestles cozily in his right hand coat
pocket, the latter being lined with velvety buckskin to prevent the hammer from catching and frustrating his purpose of converting his enemies
into full fledged angels…His language reaches out and grasps the irre-
sistible and terrible in nature, lifting it, as the Titans lifting the mountains, and lining it with awful force against those who listened to him. I
have seen him leap upon a billiard table and shout his defiance in the following stirring manner: 'Here I am again, a mile wide and all wool. I
weigh a ton, and when I walk, the earth shakes. Give me room and I'll
whip an army. I'm a blizzard from Bitter Creek. I was born in a powder
house, and raised in a gun factory. I'm bad from the bottom up, and grit
plumb through…I'm dry! Whose treat is it? Don't all speak at once for
I'll turn loose and scatter death and destruction…your treat, is it? Well,
stand in, boys. The Red Headed Woodpecker from Cow Creek is going
to liquidate'…"'The Bad Man From Bodie' is drifting down into the valley. He is located in the metropolitan centers where he may enjoy life
without the inconvenience of always dreading a vigilante committee, that
mushrooming tribunal of justice from which there is no appeal…Besides,
the winters in Bodie are very severe…'The Bad Man From Bodie'…occa-
sionally dies with his boots on, but never within the memory of man has
one been hung by a civilized hangingman. He may accidentally drop
down to oblivion through the instrumentality of an 18-inch
Bowie…When the warm weather beguiles the flitting swallow back to his
last year's nest, the 'Bad Man From Bodie' will return to his stamping
ground up in the high Sierra or again to the wilds of southwestern
Nevada. His lungs will once more expand with oath burdening winds, his
cheery voice will ring out defiance to the trembling auditors. The short
sharp yelp of his Derringer or Whistler will send the echoes flying, and
the people of the camp where he takes up his abode will smile grimly and
rub their palms as they remark in sotto voce tones, 'Wreckoes gonna live
it up this spring. I see the bone breakers got in.' The undertaker dusts out
his gorgeous death wagon…The coroner gets ready his jury lists and
makes a bargain with a particular physician in regards to holding of the
autopsies. The grave digger buys a new spade, and the man whose job is
epitaphs for dead men on imperishable marble lays in a stock of new chis-
els."[2]

Those in Bodie who committed crimes seldom felt the sting of the law, with the exception of Joseph "Frenchy" DaRoche. In DaRoche's case the "law" actually turned out to be "Judge Lynch," the Bodie 601. Bodie citizens, until then, had become indifferent to the many shootings, muggings (garroting, as it was known in Bodie), thefts, etc. in the town.

Prostitution in Bodie thrived, mainly because only about 10 per cent of the town's population consisted of women. The demand for female companionship by the men of the town far exceeded the number of ladies available. As a result, an area of the town referred to as "Bonanza Street" became a red light district. The most notable of Bodie's many prostitutes was a woman known as "Rosa May." There were a number of others who plied their trade, too, and several were somewhat famous.

These included Rosa Olague, known in the Bodie newspapers as "The Castilian Cyprian" and "Spanish Maid." Eleanor Dumont began her career in prostitution as a gambler. She was more familiarly known as "Madame Mustache." Another was known as "French Joe." Others were Ellen Fair, Nellie Monroe, Julia Hoffman, the "Belle of Eureka," who held the record for arrests and time in jail; Mademoiselle Albisue, Kittie Willis, Belle West, Kate Wise, and many, many more.

Wedertz writes: "In its infancy, Bodie supported a Maiden Lane, whose presence and mysterious atmosphere attracted the notice of J. Ross Browne in 1864. By 1879 journalists occasionally referred to the narrow street that paralleled Main Street along the west side of town from King Street to the hills to the north, as Virtue Street, Virgin Avenue, and Bonanza Street. The street appears as Virgin Avenue on Goodson's 1880 map of Bodie District, and it had become somewhat of a landmark. The ironic epithet 'Bonanza' eventually triumphed; but whatever the name, the location and the business conducted there remained the same as long as the camp prospered."[3]

As mentioned, one of Bodie's most famous ladies of the night was Rosa May. A book written about her entitled, "Rosa May: The Search for a Mining Camp Legend," was based upon a search by the author, George Williams, III, to find Rosa May's final resting place and to determine the location of her death and the facts about her life.

Williams writes that Rosa May is buried outside the confines of the Bodie Cemetery because of her occupation. The ladies of the town objected to her remains being located within the cemetery proper.

AS SEEN FROM THE "DEADHOUSE": This photo taken through a
hole in a wall of the Bodie Cemetery Deadhouse indicates the interment
location of the town's most famous prostitute, Rosa May. She is buried outside the cemetery because the town's social leaders forbad her burial within
the cemetery proper. (A Jim Watson photo)

Williams was unable to determine where Rosa May died. He states: "I
spent an entire morning searching the indexes of death and land records.
I did not find a single reference to Rosa May. As far as Mono County
records went, Rosa May had never owned land nor died in Bodie.
Evidently a negligent physician years ago failed to notify authorities of
Rosa's death or perhaps authorities hadn't cared to list the death of a prostitute. Then again, I had recently learned of two disastrous fires in Bodie,
in 1892 and 1932. Perhaps a death record at Bodie was destroyed in one
of these fires. But county clerks assured me, all of Bodie's public records
had always been kept at Bridgeport. If Rosa May died in Bodie, county
records should bear proof. But they didn't," he concluded.[4]

Ironically, the authors encountered the exact same problem when
attempting to determine all the facts in researching material in Chapter
10, "The Avalanches of 1911." A total of nine men died in three separate
avalanches that fateful March 7, 1911—one of the nine in a slide at
Masonic, 15 miles northwest of Bodie. When the authors researched the
death certificates in the Mono County Courthouse, however, eight of the
victims were listed, but the victim of the Masonic slide, a well-known
Bridgeport businessman, Samuel M. Smith, was not included.

The newspapers of the day thoroughly reported the tragedy, including his death as well as the funeral services that followed, held under the auspices of the Masonic Lodge. The authors checked the Bridgeport Cemetery and a headstone stands over his grave, of which a photo is included in this book. The authors surmise that even though Rosa May's death is not recorded in the Mono County records, this does not rule out the fact that her death could somehow have been inadvertently omitted from the records, as was the death of Smith, especially since Rosa May apparently died during this same period. Williams states in his book:

"I was pleased to find two people who had seen Rosa May, and pleased to learn that she had lived as late as 1910..."[5] Again, ironically, the authors found the listings of two 1910 deaths included in the 1911 death records section, including the 1911 avalanche victims who succumbed in March of that year. Unfortunately, neither of the two 1910 listings was Rosa May. And why the 1910 deaths were listed among those of 1911 is unknown.

During a 1994 interview with one of the authors, Doug Brodie, Mrs. Loretta Gray, 93, a Bodie native residing in Oakland, California, who has since died, recalled that as a girl she waited tables in the dining room of Bodie's Occidental Hotel operated by her mother, Mrs. Annie S. Miller. Mrs. Gray said some of the regular customers were Bodie prostitutes and she remembered them as kind and good-hearted women. She said she had no recollection of anyone named "Rosa May."[6]

One of the authors also talked to a former Bodieite who did remember seeing Rosa May sometime around 1910. Jim Watson, while discussing Bodie history with the late Mrs. Anna DeChambeau McKenzie in 1989, was told that she remembered seeing Rosa May in Bodie when Mrs. McKenzie was a young girl of 12 or 13. Mrs. McKenzie was born in 1896 on the DeChambeau family ranch at Mono Lake.[7]

To continue our review of Bodie's "Bad Men" (and women), we find that crime occasionally flourished in the minority areas of Bodie, too. The town, in its heyday, had a Chinese population of over 350. The 1880 census states the number of Chinese that year was 357. In addition, other Chinese resided in the hills between Bodie and Bridgeport where they harvested firewood for Bodie's mills and dwellings and were never counted in the census.

The Chinese in Bodie established their homes and businesses along King Street, most coming from Virginia City in 1878. A good many

Californians in those days made it clear they did not want the Chinese in "their" state. As a result, the Chinese tended to stay together maintaining their own culture and dialects.

STAGECOACH HEADQUARTERS: This is a photo of the Grand Central Hotel in 1880. The six-horse coach pulled the run between Bodie and Carson City with driver Big Tom Petit and beside him is Old Wardy, Wells Fargo shotgun messenger. George Finney is handling the four-horse team which made the trip to Virginia City. Shotgun for him was Charles Daniels at his rear. Leaning on the hotel balcony is Samuel Southworth and the lady is Mrs. Chestnut, hotel landlady. I. Stopddard Penfield stands at the head of the white horse. (Courtesy California State Library)

Crime among Bodie's Chinese was a problem in 1879. Opium dens along King Street gained notoriety and Bodie residents other than Chinese began frequenting these places. As a result of opium use, several murders occurred in the dens and in 1881 the law began making itself felt. As Bodie began a period of decline in 1882, the problem diminished. In 1883 few dens were still in business and in 1885 the Mono County Grand Jury ordered any remaining opium dens closed by law.

The town was also home to about 200 Mexican immigrants, and the 1880 census count also listed 35 Indian residents. Most, if not all, were Piaute. Several small Indian bands were located in the area surrounding Bodie. Few reports were made of trouble involving Indians and those that were listed usually involved overindulgence of alcoholic beverages.

As for the crime problem among Mexican immigrant residents, it never equaled that of the Chinese. The Mexican immigrants had no particular section of the town. They worked mainly as teamsters and wood-packers. McGrath writes: "There was no organized violence directed at Mexicans in Bodie, nor does any Mexican seem to have been attacked simply because he was a Mexican."[8]

Several shootings involving Mexicans and "gringos" did occur, but generally these involved liquor in local saloons. McGrath adds: "Mexicans also had violent confrontations with other Mexicans in Bodie. Although weapons were normally used in these fights, only one death occurred."[9]

Only a few blacks ever resided in Bodie and just one incident involving a crime can be found. It was a confrontation between a black man who reportedly attempted to stab a cook in a chop shop (restaurant), and was unsuccessful. He disappeared and no arrest was ever made.

As bad as Bodie appeared to be, the Mammoth City Times of December 17, 1879, indicated Bodie would not be a bad place to live in comparison to San Francisco. We quote the Times:

"Anybody who doesn't think that San Francisco is a pretty live village should read the list of events furnished by the local columns of the morning papers today. It comprises an attack upon a Chinese rag-picker by a band of hoodlums, a burglary on a candy store, an inquest on a murdered Mongolian, another on a suicide found in Golden Gate Park, an escape from jail, a raid on an opium den, a stabbing affray on Barbary coast, two fires, the arrest of a 16-year-old boy for attempting to murder a grocer whom he had robbed, the arrest of a woman who had attempted to cut her throat, the arrest of a felonious physician, a highway robbery by a nine-year-old boy, and a number of minor offenses. These, together with the performance of 'Lucrezia Borgia' at the Baldwin Theater by a scratch troupe, make up a catalogue of crime and disaster that is sufficiently alarming—S.F. Stock Exchange, Dec. 12. No thank you, we'd rather live in Bodie." (Comment by Times)[10]

Myrick, in his book on railroads, talks about stagecoach holdups on the roads leading to Bodie:

"Bodie became filled with idle and destitute men, and visitors were urged to keep a sharp lookout for garroters. Stages were frequently stopped. Two men, Jones and Sharp, held up seven stages in four months. At Sweetwater Station, in the early part of June, 1880, a stage was held up, the Wells Fargo box was taken, and five passengers were relieved of their valuables. A week later the same men held up the same stage at the same place and Charlie Cambridge, the driver, on recognizing the men told them he would appreciate the return of his watch because of its sentimental value. Although the return was promised, no record was ever made of the physical delivery of the property."[11]

FOOTNOTES — CHAPTER 12

1. E.H. Clough, Sacramento Bee, June 1, 1878

2. Ibid, October 16, 1880

3. Wedertz, Page 28

4. George Williams III, "Rosa May: A Search for A Mining Camp Legend," page 36

5. Ibid, page 68

6. Interview with Mrs. Loretta Gray, 1994

7. Interview with Mrs. Anna McKenzie, 1989

8. McGrath, Page 140

9. Ibid, page 142

10. Mammoth City Times, December 17, 1879

11. Myrick, Page 306

CHAPTER 13

ONLY BODIE SPOKEN HERE

Bodie humor of 1882 is just as funny today as it was more than 120 years ago. Many of the following, some news items, some items of humor, and some personal recollections, offer a view of what life was like in that small mining town:

This story ran in the Bodie Evening Miner May 23, 1882:

Mrs. Catherine Brown of San Francisco refused to pay for an oyster stew because it was sour. The restaurant man said he wouldn't have cared if Mrs. Brown hadn't eaten the stew.[1]

- - -

HUMOR—A young Bodie married man says the fellow is lucky who has his will contested only after death. He says his will has been contested ever since he got married.—May 20, 1882, Evening Miner.[2]

- - -

This story appeared in the May 29 edition: The wife of a United States Senator says that her bill for flowers during the session is $2,000. As a Senator's salary is only $6,000, this leaves the old man very little for whiskey.[3]

- - -

IMPORTANT TO BODIEITES—An English physician says a man can stop a fit of sneezing by crawling down stairs head first. Almost anything can be cured that way if the stairs are steep enough.—July 22, 1882.[4]

- - -

TOO BAD—This morning while on his rounds young Teddy Brodigan lost his water. We could learn no particulars of the disaster further than that his plug popped out and his water ran to the ground. For the information of readers outside of Bodie it is perhaps necessary to state that young Teddy belongs to the House of Brodigan which furnishes water to the people of Bodie by a system of carts.—The Evening Miner, June 24, 1882. [5]

- - -

THE MINING INDEX: Mr. Wagner stands in front of Bodie's "Mining Index," checking the latest edition in this 1906 photo. Bodie newspapers are a constant source of information about the town and Mono County. (By permission of the Eastern California Museum)

NO, YOUNG MAN, NO—A Bodie youth, signing himself "Sweet William" desired THE MINER to candidly inform him whether it hurts a young man to sow his wild oats. No, Sweet William, no; it doesn't hurt you a particle to sow your wild oats. Go ahead and sow as many as you wish; but it is the gathering in of the crop that will make you howl. And you have to gather it, too. If you don't it gathers you; and one is a great deal worse than the other. Go on, Billy, and sow your wild oats—but you just keep away from THE MINER office at harvest time. May 29, 1882. [6]

THE FIRST NEWSPAPER

The first newspaper published in Mono County, California, actually wasn't printed in Mono County nor in California but rather in the newly established Nevada Territory and before any counties had yet been authorized in the territory. The Esmeralda Star came off the press for the first time May 10, 1862 in Aurora, 16 miles east of the townsite of Bodie.

Aurora at that time served as the county seat of Mono County. The following year, however, a survey of the boundary that separated the State of California and the Territory of Nevada determined Aurora was actually 3-1/2 miles inside Nevada. Nevada legislators then established a county, named it Esmeralda, and made Aurora the county seat. That meant the first newspaper in Mono County was actually printed in Esmeralda County in Nevada Territory, not in Mono County, California.

- - -

In Bodie's quest for entertainment, the town, with the aid of donations, built a horse racing track in an area called "Brooker Flat" located at the south end of the community. It was a 600-yard oval, and within a year horse racing had become an important sporting event in Bodie. Today's visitors can see the barely discernable outline of the track from the hill on State Route 270 as it overlooks Bodie on the right—to the south of town. "The Sport of Kings" was still popular in Bodie as late as the early 1900's. The late Kent DeChambeau of Sacramento, a scion of Bodie's DeChambeau Hotel family, told the authors in an interview that Mono Lake water was used to treat cuts on horses' legs. Horse owners would transport their steeds to the lake and walk them through the water which they also believed was unique in curing split hooves.[7]

- - -

The Bodie Railway & Lumber Company, established in 1881, hired many employees during construction of the 32-1/2 miles of track and many were Indians—most of them Piautes. All but a few lived in Mono Mill, the south terminal of the railroad.

- - -

Due to often extreme cold in Bodie during winter, and the deep snow and icing of road rights-of-way, drayers developed what they termed "horse snowshoes" composed of steel plate 10 inches square and fitted with a clamp. These were attached to each of the horse's hooves. Slots were cut in the plate enabling the "shoe" to engage the calks of the standard horseshoe. This prevented the "snowshoe" from slipping off the hoof. Horse "snowshoes" in later years were wood squares and leather pads fashioned from old belting taken from the mills and nailed to the horses' hooves.

- - -

Drilling for oil occurred in the Mono Lake region from 1908 to 1910, without success. The first well was sunk on Paoha Island in Mono Lake, the larger of the two islands. After reaching a depth of 1,500 feet, drilling was abandoned when only hot water was found. A second well was drilled on the north shore, on the DeChambeau Ranch. Again only hot water resulted. A third well was drilled on the Carnonica Ranch near the foot of Cottonwood Canyon, nine miles from the lake, again with negative results.

- - -

Bodie and Mono County were subject to earthquakes during the Bodie boom years, just as today. The Mammoth and Mono areas are shaken constantly as the result of several very active faults. This story appeared in the Mammoth City Times November 8, 1879 edition: "At Aurora on the 5th, a severe shock of earthquake was felt. Court was in session at the time, and after learning what the shock was, considerable excitement was manifested..." (It must have been interesting to have been down working in those mines during an earthquake.)[8]

- - -

A huge explosion shook Bodie to its foundation the evening of July 8, 1879, when the Giant Powder Company powder magazine exploded at the old Standard works on the hill. Every boarding house and miner's cabin within the vicinity was destroyed and property damage was widespread. The shock was felt in Bridgeport 20 miles away. Seven persons were killed at the blast scene and several died later. More than 30 were injured.

- - -

A PILE OF ROCKS—Round rocks from the ocean depths off Norway played an important part in Bodie in the milling process that separated gold from ore, according to Kent DeChambeau. He explained the rocks were used by the Norwegians as ballast for their ships. When the ships were loaded with goods in San Francisco Bay the ballast would be dumped, but someone determined that because the rocks were extremely hard and almost perfectly round they could be used in the milling process to grind gold ore. As a result, they were hauled to Bodie and used in the grinding until they would become so small they were of no value and were discarded outside the mills. DeChambeau said he had seen some of these vestiges among the remains of old mills in the Bodie area.[9]

— — —

DeChambeau also informed the authors of the little-known gathering of approximately 6,000 Chinese in Bodie during the years 1902-1903. These Chinese came together in Bodie during this two-year period after the decline of gold and silver mining at the turn of the century. They remained in Bodie for this short period apparently to discuss their future endeavors and they gradually departed in 1903 until only a few remained. As he explained, probably most took the trail that led back to their homeland. Their goal was not permanent residency in California nor Nevada. They intended to stay only until they earned enough money to provide them a respected and secure place in Chinese society in their homeland. They were sojourners rather than immigrants, and, as such, had no intention of becoming Americanized. Only a few learned English or adopted Western style dress. For the most part, they stayed clustered in Chinatowns and, except through work, had little contact with the American society at large.[10]

A FAMILIAR STREET SCENE: Before electricity reached Bodie, this scene of donkeys packing firewood into the town was common. Bodie needed huge supplies of wood to fuel the stamp mills, heat the citizen's houses as well as wood for shoring up mines. Indians supplied most of the wood by donkey. (By permission of the Eastern California Museum)

— — —

AND, FROM THE FEBRUARY 26, 1881 BRIDGEPORT CHRONICLE-UNION: DANCING ACADEMY—Capt. G.L. Porter has been prevailed upon to open a dancing school here, and is meeting with great success—having a large class and giving general satisfaction. (11)

- - -

Bodie was proud of its one-armed lawyer, Pat Reddy, who was considered an all-round fine man, generous to a fault. From the March 24, 1881 Bridgeport Chronicle-Union:

THE HOUSE OF PAT REDDY: Pat Reddy, a one-armed criminal lawyer was known throughout the West. His reputation was based upon his ability to defend the criminal element in addition to union members and the underdog. He was elected a State Senator in 1882. This house stands at union and Prospect Streets. (A Jim Watson photo)

GENEROUS—Upon the acquittal of Morton, in the Superior Court, he remarked to the court that he had been eight months in jail, and was destitute: whereupon the Hon. P. Reddy, prosecuting attorney, quietly handed him a $20 piece. This is in keeping with his well-known generosity.(12)

And, from the Bodie Evening Miner of November 10, 1882:

Pat Reddy was elected California State Senator Tuesday, November 6. He arrived back in Bodie today.(13)

- - -

Another well-known Bodieite, Judge J.G. McClinton, luckily escaped from this accident with his life. From the October 22, 1879 Mammoth City Times:

VEHICLE ACCIDENT OF THE DAY—On Friday evening, a short distance from town, the whittletree (also refered to as "Whiffletree" and "Whippletree") of Judge McClinton's buggy broke, the neckyoke came off and the tongue fell to the ground, which, throwing the vehicle upon the horses, caused them to run. The judge was thrown out and the wheel passed over his chest. He was not seriously hurt.[14]

- - -

From the Bodie Evening Miner in 1882:
TREE GROWERS—Many Bodieites have planted willows near their residences without success, during the past three years. Caspar Belmont and James Aylward, on Standard Avenue, have made a new departure. These gentlemen brought in a number of small pines from Rough Creek, and planted them in front of their houses, and they are growing nicely. Here is something for our home artists to ponder over. (Authors: But, alas, we know the only thing green that ever grew in Bodie was hops.)[15]

- - -

Again, from the Evening Miner in 1882:
IMPROVEMENTS—Main Street is undergoing some necessary improvements. A drain is being dug along the east side, from Hoffman's up to THE MINER office; while a branch is run across the street from the Occidental Hotel toward the Rifle Club Saloon, which will tap the springs that have made this portion of Main Street so miry. Well, Bodie ought to have a good street; there has been enough road tax paid by her citizens to put a Belgian pavement on Main Street from one end of it to the other.[16]

- - -

From the Miner, 1882:
SHARKS—Sharks are reported numerous in Mono Lake. This will interfere with the pleasures of bathing in that inland sea this summer. [17]

- - -

Few if any readers of this publication, we are sure, have ever heard of "THE UNIVERSAL BENEVOLENT ASSOCIATION FOR UNMAR-RIED PERSONS." The Bodie Evening Miner, in the 1880's, often carried advertisements for that organization, and they read as follows:

Co-operative Life Insurance and Marriage Endowment; Northwestern Masonic Aid Association; Home Benefit Association and Accident Class. Preferred Limit, $5,000—$25 Weekly Indemnity; Ordinary Limit, $4,000—$20 Weekly Indemnity; Medium Limit, $3,000—$15 Weekly Indemnity. L.N. Snyder, Agent, Bodie, office at Taylor's Billiard Parlor, next to Stewart's Drug Store.

This story accompanied the advertisement:

MARRIAGE ENDOWMENT—In marrying it is quite necessary to have some of the wherewith to meet the emergencies of that state. All unmarried persons, old and young, of both sexes, can avail themselves of the benefits of this mutual plan, and by an occasional small outlay lay the foundation of a comfortable competency. The institution is on the mutual benevolent plan. By paying your dues, if you marry inside of one, two or three years you receive at marriage a sum of money ranging from $500 to $2,000, according to the endowment policy taken out. L.N. Snyder is the agent in Bodie and has his office at A.M. Taylor's, next door to Stewart's drug store.[18]

- - -

There has been the question as to whether Bodieites ever got fresh milk. The answer is a decided yes, and as an indication of this, the following are stories regarding dairies in those early days.

From the Bodie Evening Miner in 1882.

- - -

A SAD CALAMITY VISITS A WORTHY MAN—Last night the cow stables on the milk ranch of Jerome Smith, located in the north end of town, were totally destroyed by fire. Out of twenty-three milch cows stabled in the buildings seventeen perished in the flames. The scene of the conflagration was so remote that our firemen were unable to reach the spot in time to save anything, although the department was promptly on the ground. This is a sad financial blow to Jerome, who has struggled hard for years to build up a business in Bodie, and had but recently succeeded in freeing himself from debt. There was no insurance on the property.[19]

THE TEN COMMANDMENTS: Until vandals made off with this large oilcloth listing of the Ten Commandments, visitors who entered the Bodie Methodist Church could view this interesting scroll above the pulpit. The church now is closed to visitors who must peer through screening.
(A Jim Watson photo)

- - -

From the Miner issue of May 20, 1882:
THE BOVINE CHORUS—The somewhat unusual serenade which awakened residents from their slumbers at sunrise this morning was nothing so very remarkable, after all. The bovine chorus simply came from the throats of the large herd of milch cows belonging to the Moresi Brothers, which were being removed from their winter quarters near Bodie, to the large dairy ranch at the mouth of Cottonwood Canyon. A sort of farewell bellow, as it were.[20]

- - -

A very successful soft drink manufacturing firm, called a soda water factory in Bodie's early days, was Pearson Brothers. Bottles from this business are highly sought after today. The following two stories regarding this business ran in the Bodie Evening Miner in 1882:
ENTERPRISE—The Pearson Bros., at the Soda Factory, are about to add to the supply of water in the town. They are digging a drain in which to lay pipe from a spring back of the factory down Lowe and through Main Street; and they intend running a tunnel into the hillside to find a

larger supply of water than the spring affords at present. Bodie has the best water in the mountains.[21]

- - -

MORE WATER—In the rear of their soda factory the Pearson Brothers have built a stone reservoir with a capacity of three thousand gallons, from which they will soon begin to furnish the people of Bodie with pure water. They are now building a house over the reservoir. (22)

- - -

News items from newspapers dating from Bodie's heyday in the late 1870's through the years up to the present offer a broad perspective of life in and around the community.

Mono Lake, wrote Mark Twain, "Is a lifeless, treeless, hideous desert, eight thousand feet above the level of the sea, and is guarded by mountains two thousand feet higher, whose summits are always clothed in clouds. This solemn, silent, sailless sea—this lonely tenant of the loneliest spot on earth—is little graced with the picturesque."[23]

But J. Ross Browne, author, artist and noted humorist of the 1860's, described the same place, but in these words:

It well deserves the name suggested by an early visitor, "Dead Sea of the West." Not even that wondrous sea, whose bitter waters wash the ruined sites of Sodom and Gomorrah, presents a scene of greater desolation…. Yet for grandeur of scenery, and for interesting geological phenomena, this lake of the Western Sierras is far superior to the Oriental Sea. Here the traveler, whether artist, geologist, botanist, or poet, might spend many months, and find ample occupation for every hour of his time.[24]

- - -

Quite often included in publications about Bodie, are references to men in leadership positions who carry the title of "judge." Browne, who served as a correspondent for Harper's New Monthly Magazine, a national periodical of those early days, in a series of articles about Bodie and Mono Lake in 1863, told of taking a short trip from Aurora to the then partially developed mining camp of Bodie with a new acquaintance who drove the horse and buggy. He wrote, "My friend was called 'The Judge', though I believe he claimed to be no higher rank than an attorney at law.

All popular lawyers, however, are judges in Nevada, whether they prac-
tice at the bar or sit upon the bench."(25)

- - -

Serving as Harper's correspondent was a prestigious role and Bodie's
citizenry was impressed with Browne's position, so much so that they told
him the main street would be named after him. Browne wrote: "Some of
the city dignitaries, however, duly impressed with the importance of having a view of their town appear in the illuminated pages of 'Harper' paid
me the compliment to attach my name to the principal street; and thus,
in future ages, I confidently expect my memory will be rescued from
oblivion." Browne, in one of his pen and ink impressions of the mining
town of the 1860's for publication, included a scene entitled, "Browne
Street, Bodie."(26)

- - -

In his book "Bodie Bonanza," Warren Loose, a second generation
Bodieite (his father and two uncles settled in Bodie in 1876 and 1877)
quoted Browne's words and then added his own: "Alas, for the transitory
memory and short-lived enthusiasm of the early city fathers of Bodie! I,
who am a second-generation Bodieite, must sadly admit that no street
map of Bodie bears the name of that illustrious journalist."(27)

This is true, at least insofar as the 1881 map of the town. The authors
checked a copy of this map in the Mono County Courthouse in
Bridgeport. No Browne Street appears. However, Frank S. Wedertz, in
his book "Bodie 1859-1900" includes a photograph on Page 183, with
the accompanying caption:

"Mrs. Elizabeth Ann (Butler) Kernohan, the first woman to live in
Bodie. The Kernohan residence was one of the first in the camp and
(Mono) county records place its location on Browne Street, which was
named for J. Ross Browne. Other miners, Krouse and Reese, had a house
on Browne Street in 1869. The spring at the west end of Browne Street
fed the 12 stamp Homestake Mill. Photo taken in 1864."(28)

And so, J. Ross Browne, your name has been rescued from oblivion as
you so confidently expected, although not as the name of Bodie's main
street, because that thoroughfare carries the name "Main Street" to this
day.

- - -

The Bodie Volunteer Fire Department in 1892 had a problem with, of all things, fire. A copy of the minutes of October of that year; "Regular meeting of Bodie Board of Fire Delegates members present, Chairman Gorman and Chairman pro-tem Nepheston: Reading of the previous minutes of the last regular meeting of the Board (July, 1892) was dispensed with as the records were destroyed by fire July, 1892."

- - -

During Bodie's peak year of 1879 the old axiom "streets paved with gold" was almost a fact. For instance, this article of Saturday, November 8, 1879 from the Bodie Chronicle:

STANDARD MILL: Described as the most inspiring structure in Bodie, this is the second mill built on this site. The first, a wood structure, built in 1877, burned in 1898. This present 20-stamp mill a corrugated iron building, was built immediately thereafter. It featured a 2,500-foot tramway that ran up the slope of Bodie Bluff. It was developed by A.S. Hallidie, the inventor of the San Francisco cable car system. (A Jim Watson photo)

"THE BODIE MINES—SPAULDING (name of a mine): A contract has been closed by the Spaulding Company with John N. Risdon, of the Risdon Iron Works, San Francisco, for the immediate erection of a ten-stamp quartz mill. The mill is to be furnished with steel boilers and be first-class in all its appointments, and be in running order in 90 days from commencement of work, and will cost $88,000. It is the intention of the company to run the mill on custom ore until their own mine is sufficiently developed to give it constant employment.

"...ground for the new mill was broken on Wednesday morning and to the surprise of all a ledge of fine looking quartz was unearthed about a foot from the surface and showing a width of at least six feet. This ledge looks very promising and can be traced the entire length of the Spaulding ground and doubtless to an indefinite length south."[29]

- - -

And from the same newspaper issue, another article:

"DECIDEDLY RICH—The Standard is undoubtedly the 'boss' gold mine, and its richness may be judged from what a knowing one says of it, that when a mass of ore is thrown down a man can scrape up enough of the loose dust to enable him to get away with $5,000 in his lunch bucket in three days. What a glorious place that big hole in the ground is for a light fingered gentleman to work in!"[30]

- - -

Another indication of the richness of the ore mined during the peak period was a report by D.M. Riordan, superintendent of the Syndicate Mill from 1878 to 1880, as quoted by Loose in "Bodie Bonanza:" "...During the crushing of this ore, so rich was it,...we have had the amalgam accumulate in the pans, not once, but frequently, so that it would stop the engine...I would take off the screen to find that the gold had accumulated in the bottom of the mortar until it was flush with the die."[31]

- - -

The importance of a water supply was made evident in an article from the November 8, 1879 Bodie Chronicle issue: "WATER SUPPLY—Today the bids for building a reservoir on the 'hill' and laying pipe to supply water for the extinguishment of fires in our town will be opened, and probably a contract let by the Bodie Water Company, a sufficient amount having been subscribed to warrant the company in pushing the good work to speedy completion. When the contemplated supply is furnished our city will be as well protected against the devouring element as is any place of its size in the state." (That reservoir, near the old railroad depot, remains to this day, fed by a spring.)

"With two hose carts, each with from 500 to 750 feet of hose, and about 1,000 feet of spare hose in case of an emergency, no fire could get under any headway. The day that sees the completion of this important work will be a memorable one to Bodie, as it will abolish the slavery we are squirming under—the fetters that bind us to the insurance companies of San Francisco and the East would be sundered and we freed from an onerous bondage; and thousands of dollars will be kept within the confines of Bodie that now go to those companies.

"…next to the extinguishment of fires, the extinguishment of the dust on our streets, and which had made life in Bodie almost unendurable is no small item in itself, and this alone should make the average Bodieite daily offer up a prayer for the speedy consummation of the good work."[32]

The firm Gilson and Barber, operators of Bodie's largest general merchandise store, was awarded the contract for providing and laying the pipe. It was placed in ditches three feet deep and when the pipe was covered, several inches of stable manure was placed on top of the pipe to prevent it from freezing. The job was completed January 14, 1880 at a cost of $16,000. The newspaper also reported two hose carts had arrived from San Francisco complete with 1,000 feet of hose and were placed in operation for use by the newly-created Champion and Neptune hose companies.

- - -

The Standard Mill, that imposing structure that remains as a feature of Bodie State Historic Park, actually is the second such mill to be built on the same site. The first, a wood structure, was destroyed by fire in 1898, and the present 20-stamp mill, a corrugated iron building, was erected immediately thereafter. A newspaper reporter in 1879 described the mill as "The most imposing structure that could be seen from Bodie's Main Street." It opened July 10, 1877, and in the first 13 months produced 43,295 ounces of gold which sold then for $30 per ounce, a value of $1,298,850, or, in terms of today's dollars at $400 an ounce, $17,318,000.

A reporter described the mill and its operations. One of the features, he said, was a tramway that extended 2,500 feet up the slope of Bodie Bluff from the Standard Mill to the mine. The tramway was developed by A.S. Hallidie, the inventor of the San Francisco cable car system. In November, 1877, he announced he had signed a contract to erect his endless ropeway in Bodie to carry ore. It went into operation in February, 1878 and consisted of 5,000 feet of 5/8-inch cable hung on towers 150 feet apart. These supported the cables to which were attached, 100 feet apart, 50 ore buckets each of three tons capacity. (Authors: it is believed this is an exaggeration) The bucket bottoms were hinged and an arm was tripped at the mill to release the contents. The cable hung 20 feet above the hillside and power was delivered from a steam engine at the mill until 1893 when electricity was delivered from the new Green Creek Power Plant. A total of 45 tons of ore was transported each eight-hour shift and offered the advantage of ore delivery even during the winter. A problem was the stretching of the cable because of ore weight. After operating for three months in 1879, the system was halted and 23 feet of slack removed from the line. Delivery of 1,300 to 1,500 tons of ore per month continued for ten years.

Author Doug Brodie, a native of British Columbia, Canada, during a recent visit there, discovered remarkable similarities between Bodie and the City of Nelson, B. C. Both began as mining towns. Nelson was the first municipality in British Columbia to operate its own power plant, begun in 1896 and completed in 1899. J.S. Cain established the Green Creek plant just three years earlier, in 1893.

In 1895 a nine-mile aerial cable tramway, extending from the Silver King Gold Mine to the Nelson Smelter at Rosemont was built by the same Mr. A.S. Hallidie, working as the California Wireworks Company of San Francisco, who erected Bodie's two mile long Standard Mill tramway in 1878. It operated by gravity. The Canadian project was begun in October 1895 and completed January 1, 1896. It also operated by gravity. It was supported by 123 wooden towers. The cable held 875 buckets of 150 to 175 pounds each, delivering 10 tons of ore each day.

- - -

Wedertz noted the Bodie mines produced about $21 million dollars worth of gold and silver, half of which came from the Standard. "It operated profitably for at least 30 years and has to be included among the best gold mines in the world." This would equal $280 million at today's prices. Not bad for one little old mining camp.

- - -

In a more modern vein the quarterly newspaper, "Out West," winter issue, 1989, in an article entitled "Bad Luck Bodie," it was indicated it might be bad luck to carry off articles from the ghost town. Editor/Publisher Chuck Woodbury wrote: "If you visit the California ghost town of Bodie, don't steal a souvenir. It's illegal to remove an historic artifact—from a rock to a rusty nail. But even if the law doesn't spot your crime, you may end up in trouble. Some people claim that if you steal something from Bodie, you'll be cursed with bad luck.

"'One woman sent some stuff back after 30 years,' said park employee Susan Des Baillets. 'She said it affected her luck. We just got a packet of nails returned to us from France.

" 'We get nails mailed to us all the time, even rocks.'

"Here's what a few folks wrote (with their original spelling) when returning artifacts to the California State Park: 'Hello: My dad has gotten our family mixed up with a little bad luck. He read your notes on how people have picked up things from Bodie and have had bad luck in the future. He seems not to believe it and went on to take something, like this old rusty nail. After about a week or two our car started to go crazy. What I mean is that the water leaked through the coolant system into the motor and caused the engine block to crack. Now that wright there is over $2,000 to get it fixed, since it's a German made car, but anyway, then he accidentally put his $100 glasses in a box that was going to Goodwill. Now there gone. And you know how these things always happen in threes, well the other day my Dad almost got in a car accident. Well before the thing happens to roll around we want to send your nail back, so whoever it is, and would also like to stress very strongly to the other curious people…don't take anything from Bodie because the bad luck will catch up with you. (signed) Sincerely, ???'

"'Dear Bodie: On a recent visit this summer, we found this door knocker in the fields north of your town. Ever since we took it, we've had bad luck, so we would like to return it to its home…sorry for breaking the rules. I guess we learned our lesson. Sincerely, X (The Guilty Party).'" [33]

- - -

Kent Pierce, a former Stockton/Sacramento, California television newsman and resident of Bodie three years during the 1930's, whose story is told elsewhere in this book, remembers when a letter was received from a visitor from Pennsylvania who wrote to Pierce's mother, who, at that time, was the postmistress. The writer confessed that during a visit to Bodie he had stolen a metal door to the Express Office, and was returning it because of a feeling of guilt. The door arrived several days later, C.O.D., with $200 postage due. [34]

As the rules state for visitors:

"SOUVENIRS AND COLLECTING: Everything in Bodie is part of the historic scene, and is fully protected. NOTHING may be collected or removed from the park. Metal detectors are not allowed."

- - -

A little known fact is that much land surrounding the ghost town of Bodie is owned by Barron Hilton, chairman of Hilton Hotels. In the July, 1988 issue of Nevada Magazine, Page 89, comes the following: "BARRON HILTON'S FLYING M—When most people think of Hilton, they envision high-rise hotels. But perhaps the most unique of all the Hilton properties is the 480,000-acre Flying M Ranch. Situated along 29 miles of the East Walker River, the massive ranch stretches from Mono Lake to Walker Lake and surrounds seven ghost towns, including Bodie. The main ranch house is about 25 miles from Yerington.

"There, Barron Hilton, chairman of Hilton Hotels, has co-mingled the working outfit with what its promotional material calls an 'exclusive conference facility' that provides 'a magnificent retreat in one of the country's true 'last frontiers'. Hundreds of guests come to the ranch each year, usually by air. They land at its mile-long jet strip and are taken to the main house, which doubles as a conference center for up to 18 visitors at a time. Every other year Hilton uses the ranch to host the Barron Hilton Soaring Club, which attracts some of the world's foremost soaring pilots and enthusiasts, including the event's founder and namesake."[35]

- - -

An 1879 newspaper item: "The Bodie Committee of Safety has issued a stirring address to the public concerning the matter of stovepipes"...and another: "The News" says Bodie is improving wonderfully. The noise of saw and hammer rebounds from daylight till dark, telling the story of improvement. All over town the work is going on. Mills, hoisting works, stores and dwelling houses are going up on every hand with the greatest rapidity"...and another: "The Standard says that

Messrs. G.L. Porter & Co., lumber dealers, have constructed a sail boat to navigate Mono Lake with a view of bringing lumber across from the north side of Leevining Creek to a point on the Bodie side of the lake about ten miles from town."

1906 BODIE BASEBALL TEAM: Two members in this photo can be identified. The man at the right rear is William B. Evans Sr. Mrs. Catherine Mathison of Carson City, NV identifies her great-uncle Will Smith bottom row-center, a Bodie barber at the time the photo was taken in front of his Bodie Barber Shop. Evans Sr. was father of Mono County Sheriff W.B. Evans and Superior Court Judge Walter Evans.
(Courtesy Mrs. Catherine Mathison)

‒ ‒ ‒

Sports played a key roll in Bodie as a pastime from the town's beginning. Baseball was popular. Wrestling drew many participants and spectators, alike. Racing was also popular, and involved two-footed as well as four-footed participants—Bodieites ran and walked in competition.

Most foot races were for extensive distances of 100 to 300 miles. The Daily Free Press carried a story February 25, 1881, about the only race involving female participants—two prostitutes, Daisy Livingstone and Kitty Franklin. They walked in a 10-mile indoor race before a goodly audience and Daisy won by 19 laps.[36] Bodieites also held dog fights and occasionally these involved other animals, including a badger, a bobcat, and even a bear. Pistol matches were held and there was a Bodie Rifle Club.

INDEPENDENCE DAY TUG O' WAR IN BODIE, 1905: The United States Hotel on the east side of Main Street served as an ideal arena for one of the big events in Bodie in its July 4th celebration. As the community faded with time, so did the U.S. Hotel until it finally became a victim of the 1932 fire. (By permission of the Eastern California Museum)

THE CARD OF A PROFESSIONAL HYPNOTIST: George W. Hammer was a practicing hypnotist in Bodie's boom years. His personal card, adorned with drawings, noted he would give "public and private exhibitions." (A Jim Watson photo)

- - -

Any book about Bodie would be incomplete without a reference to the oft-quoted little girl and her prayerful lament when she learned she would be leaving her home and moving to Bodie.

An 1879 issue of the Nevada Tribune quoted a sweet little three-year old living in the city of San Jose, California: "Good-bye, God; we are going to Bodie in the morning." Upon hearing this the Bodie Standard News rose to the occasion. In its February 23, 1879 issue, it printed this response: "'Goodbye, God we are going to Bodie in the morning,' was the suggestive termination of a sweet little three year old's prayer the other evening in San Jose, just prior to the departure of the family for the wicked mining camp mentioned. Not bad that; but rather severe on Bodie. All right, partner; but we have no particular use for a God that confines himself to the limits of San Jose; and we can't wonder that even a little three year old was willing to say 'Goodby,' when she thought she had a chance to get outside of that detestable place in order to come to Bodie."(37) The belligerent Bodie Daily Free Press also rose up in angry indignation when it heard about the little girl and her prayer, and responded in a slightly different manner. The Free Press stated a typographical error had occurred in the printed story and that what she really had said when told the family would move to Bodie, was: "Good! By God! We're going to Bodie!" Other published versions of the story were similar, with the exception of her home town. The sorrowful little three-year-old girl lived either in San Jose or Truckee, California; Aurora, Nevada, Bodie's "sister city," or somewhere in the far-off state of Colorado. Whatever the location, she was saying goodbye to God before making that final trip to Bodie.

- - -

The June 4, 1882 issue of the Bodie Evening Miner, carried this story: BODIE SCANDAL—A Bodie wife placed in her husband's hand this morning, as he was leaving for downtown, a note of which the following is a true copy: "I am forced to tell you something that I know will trouble you, but it is my duty to do so. I am determined you shall know it, let the result be what it may.

"I have known for a week that this trial was coming, but kept it to myself until today, when it has reached a crisis, and I cannot keep it any longer. You must not censure me too harshly, for you must reap the benefits as well as myself. I do hope it won't crush you. The flour is all out. Please send me some this afternoon. I thought by this method you would not forget it." George Gilson of the Gilson & Barber Store had a sack of flour on that lady's doorstep within thirty minutes. (38)

- - -

More Bodie humor, circa 1882.

A news note from the Bodie Evening Miner of May 15:

"Cleve has returned from the hot springs.

During his absence he bathed his feet, and feels considerably invigorated."[39]

- - -

From the May 31 Evening Minor:

"Old Settler," Bishop Creek, writes: "Please send me a cure for apple tree worms." "Well, old son, the agricultural editor of THE MINER would gladly accommodate you, but he cannot suggest a cure until he knows what ails the worms."[40]

- - -

From the May 23 issue:

A SLANDER—This story is told on a physician living not forty miles from Bodie: "One of our 'doctors,' a man of limited sense and 'limiteder' education, was called to see Mr. R's little boy, who was quite ill. He gave him some medicine and left, promising to call on the following morning. When he arrived Mr. R met him at the gate and informed him that the child was convalescent. 'Convalescent?' said the doctor, 'convalescent? Then if he is that bad off you'll have to call in some other physician; I never treated a case of that kind in my life!' and with that he mounted his horse and departed."[41]

- - -

From the June 6 Miner:

BOYS, PREPARE FOR IT—It is the fashion East for ladies to have a live bug, attached to a fine gold chain, run at large about their personage, crawling about their shoulders, and making itself at home. We do not know that this fashion will extend to Bodie, but we mention it so young men need not be astonished at anything they may find while in the company of their adored ones and show their ignorance by killing the bug. Nothing would be more apt to create a coldness between two young people than for the man to slap his girl on the bug and kill it. (42)

- - -

THE MINER, although grateful to be offered assistance by its competition following a burglary and vandalism of its offices, was begrudg-
ingly critical of the editor of the Bodie Free Press, which the MINER
often referred to as the "FREE PEE." This was a MINER story in August,
1882:

OUR THANKS—Shortly after the vandalism in THE MINER office
last Tuesday, H.Z. Osborne called on us and generously tendered any
facilities the FREE PRESS office afforded to aid in getting out our paper.
We expected no less from Mr. Osborne: and he knows us well enough to
know that the kindness would be duly appreciated and properly acknowledged without his publishing the fact on the street. The acknowledge-
ment would have been made sooner but that we would not care to say
anything about the matter while the vandal was on trial.

- - -

Bodie did not have a system of house numbering and in order to find
a dwelling or business, it was often necessary to have a description of the
location being sought. The Bodie Evening Miner masthead carried this
information: 'THE BODIE EVENING MINER, Orlando E. Jones,
Editor, John J. Curry, Founder-Publisher. Office—The large building
formerly occupied by Stevens & Smith as an auction house, next door to
T. M. Luther & Co.'s assay office, Main Street, Bodie, California—
"emphatically and uncompromisingly Democratic, the only true
National Party."

The "Orlando E. Jones" listed as editor, is the same man mentioned
in a Nevada Magazine article entitled "Mining Camp Chronicles" in the
March/April 1989 issue that describes him as a "former circus clown."
The author Jack Highton, notes: "Orlando E. Jones thought the desert
near Hawthorne would soon bloom as a metropolis. The Carson and
Colorado Railroad laid out the townsite of Hawthorne in the spring of
1881 after it opened its terminus at the south end of Walker Lake. So
Jones, expecting a boom, founded a newspaper called 'The Oasis'. As
newspaper bibliographers put it: 'Jones, a former circus clown, who
would perform for even the smallest audience, was also willing to try to
issue a paper for only a handful of subscribers. For five weeks he produced a newspaper for the cluster of shanties that would someday be
Hawthorne...Jones moved to Bodie, California where he apparently
found square meals since he ran two papers there for nearly a decade,"

and [43] one of these was the Bodie Evening Miner from which we quote several news stories about Bodie and its humor of a century ago. Jones was named editor of the newspaper when it began publication May 8, 1882.

- - -

As mining activity in Bodie began to wane in late 1882, businesses closed. One firm, "Reinstein & Wolf, Regulators," placed this large ad in the Evening Miner that year:

W A R; W A R; W A R;

To Oregon or Bust!

WE MEAN BUSINESS!

Having concluded to clearout our business we will sell everything in our line for what it will bring

Dwelling House, Store Room, Fire Proof Warehouse, everything for sale.

Our prices will compare favorably with any house in town.

- - -

President Abraham Lincoln may inadvertently have served as an advocate for the sale of whisky in Bodie, or at least one Bodie saloon believed so as evidenced by this 1882 advertisement in the Bodie Evening Miner, offered by the newspaper in the form of a news item:

SANITARY CONDITION OF BODIE

Once upon a time some one told President Lincoln that one of his Generals drank too much whisky. Old Abe immediately ordered the tattler to find out where the aforesaid General got his whisky, and to buy all of that brand he could find. "Do you think that will stop him from drinking?" asked the tattler. "No, I don't want him to stop; I want to supply my other Generals with it. It may make them better." Precisely the same article of whisky is now for sale over the bar of Peters & Aldridge's saloon, Main Street, Bodie.

- - -

One name of prominence was interwoven in the latter years of Bodie when Theodore Hoover, the brother of President Herbert Hoover, served as general manager of the Standard Mining Company. Theodore Hoover later went on to become the head of the School of Mines at Stanford

University. His famous brother visited Theodore and stayed with him in the general manager's home on the hill adjacent the Standard Mill. Still standing, the dwelling has become known as the "Hoover residence."

- - -

We all know of the famous outlaws, Jesse and Frank James. The Evening Miner carried this story in 1882:

Frank James arrived in Bodie this morning and was warmly greeted by J. H. Vincent, Joe Marshall, C.F. McKinley, N.S. Warren and E.V. Upton, and many other old time friends and schoolmates. Frank says he has no intention of avenging Jesse's death. He will probably take the lecture field as soon as the American Press have sufficiently advertised him. There is talk of giving Col. Frank James a place on the Bodie Louisiana Returning Board and retaining his efficient services in Mono County until after the election.

There is no indication that Frank James ever returned to Bodie following this visit.

FOOTNOTES — CHAPTER 13

1. Bodie Evening Miner, May 23, 1882
2. Ibid, May 20, 1882
3. Ibid, May 29, 1882
4. Ibid, July 22, 1882
5. Ibid, June 24, 1882
6. Ibid, May 29, 1882
7. Kent DeChambeau, an interview
8. Mammoth City Times, November 8, 1879
9. Kent DeChambeau, an interview
10. Ibid
11. Bridgeport Chronicle-Union, February 26, 1881
12. Ibid, March 24, 1881
13. Bodie Evening Miner, November 10, 1882
14. Mammoth City Times, October 22, 1879
15. Bodie Evening Miner, May 20, 1882
16. Ibid, June 12, 1882
17. Ibid, July 7, 1882

18. Ibid, August 6, 1882

19. Ibid, August 6, 1882

20. Ibid, September 10, 1882

21. Ibid, October 4, 1882

22. Ibid, October 4, 1882

23. Mark Twain, "Roughing It," page 243

24. J. Ross Browne, page 64

25. Ibid, page 4

26. Ibid, page 40

27. Loose, page 33

28. Wedertz, page 183

29. Bodie Chronicle-Union, November 8, 1879

30. Ibid

31. Loose, page 65

32. Bodie Chronicle, November 8, 1879

33. Out West, Winter Issue, 1989

34. Kent Pierce, an interview

35. Nevada Magazine, July, 1988, page 89

36. Bodie Daily Free Press, February 25, 1881

37. Bodie Standard News, February 13, 1879

38. Bodie Evening Miner, June 4, 1882

39. Ibid, May 15, 1882

40. Ibid, May 31, 1882

41. Ibid, May 23, 1882

42. Ibid, June 6, 1882

43. Nevada Magazine, March / April, 1989

CHAPTER 14

BODIE IN A MODERN WORLD

The Bodie of today is reminiscent of the past. It exists in a state of arrested decay as a result of the joint efforts of the J.S. Cain estate and the State of California. The Cains brought it to where it is today. The State plans to keep it that way. But it could, and it nearly did, become a much different place—a much different environment.

JIM CAIN, 1854-1939, BODIE'S PROTECTOR: James S. Cain is responsible for saving Bodie for future generations to enjoy. Prior to 1900 he purchased land as it came on the market and believed until his dying day that much Bodie gold remains. (Photo from a private collection)

Mining was about to return to Bodie in the 1990s—as late as 1997. The rewards of such an endeavor could have been mind boggling. The dollar amount in terms of gold and silver buried deep in Bodie Bluff and Standard Hill has been estimated at two billion by Mark Whitehead, a geologist employed by the now defunct Bodie Consolidated Mining Co., a subsidiary of Galactic Services, itself a subsidiary of Galactic Resources of Vancouver, B.C., Canada. Bodie Consolidated, for three years, operated an office in Bridgeport, California, 25 miles from Bodie.

"The stakes are high," the gamblers would say at the faro tables in old Bodie.

More than 140 years have passed since William S. Bodey unearthed gold that led to the formation of the mining district and town eventually named for him. The fortunes of Bodie have risen and fallen during the years since that 1859 discovery.

The processes used to mine gold and silver during the 19th Century and early in the 20th Century were far different than the open pit process of today. Yesterday's hard rock mining consisted of digging holes and tunnels into the hillsides and mountain slopes. Today's methods simply involve removing the entire hills and mountains.

Galactic proposed employing such modern mining techniques at the eastern edge of Bodie, just over Bodie Bluff, but these plans were dropped in 1992. Galactic's advocates maintained the mining activities would be out of sight and sound of the townsite of Bodie and their plan involved the historic state park—the State—and Mono County in controversy for three years. The matter was put to rest because of a problem encountered by the mining firm in another project in the State of Colorado.

An example of the modern-day process for mining gold exists just a few miles east of Bodie at the old townsite of Aurora, Nevada. Today Aurora is a huge open pit. To an observer standing at the edge of the pit looking down, a truck at the bottom looks like a toy, and the operation is based upon the "heap-leach" treatment of crushed ore.

A description of open pit mining is contained in a 1989 copy of Motorland Magazine written by John Holmgren as he viewed the Round Mountain Gold Corp. mining operation near Tonopah, Nevada.

"...Folks in Tonopah had told me about a big new mining operation in the Smoky Valley about 40 miles south of Austin. When I got my first glimpse of the place, I was flabbergasted—thought Howard Hughes had been reincarnated and decided to build a plant to hold 209 Spruce Gooses. Actually, this extensive complex of buildings and open pit mines is a fairly recent facility...it seems that gold mining has become profitable again, and parts of Nevada are literally crawling with new ventures. There are some 400 companies operating in the silver state, with a total employment of about 10,000 people.

"Round Mountain began heap-leach mining in 1970. At that time it was called the Smoky Valley Mining Co....The success of heap-leach mining is in handling large amounts of aggregate efficiently. Round Mountain processes 130,000 tons per day and is the world's largest open pit heap-leach gold mine—it produces some 300,000 ounces of gold a year, worth some $120 million."[1]

Bodie Consolidated's plans for Bodie Bluff began with the purchase of the patent rights to 550 acres adjacent to the eastern edge of Bodie Park from the international mining group known as Homestake Mining for $31 million in the 1980s. For 18 months core sample drilling was done to determine the amount of gold and silver bearing ores. This added another $3 million to the total expenditure.

GEOLOGIST MARK WHITEHEAD: Bodie Consolidated Mining Company official Whitehead and aide Steve Amundson (left) explain the geological formations of Bodie Bluff. The firm planned an open pit mining operation proposed for the early 1990's. The Company's parent firm, Galactic Resources Ltd. Of Vancouver, Canada went bankrupt in 1995, and the mining plans were cancelled. (A Jim Watson photo)

Geologist Whitehead explained during the core sample drilling period that the then-proposed mining operations would involve a combination of conventional milling and C-I-P, or carbon-in-pulp processing for the higher grade ore. The lesser grade ores would involve the heap leach, or cyanide process for larger tonnages of low grade ore. This would involve extraction of gold by grinding up the gold-bearing rock and soaking it in a cyanide solution. In the process gold particles become affixed to the cyanide and in turn this solution is drained off and the gold is extracted.

The mining company planned to locate the heap leach facilities in a basin to the east side of Bodie Bluff and Standard Hill, out of sight of visitors to Bodie, in the same location that old Bill Bodey discovered gold in 1859.

The company had planned an open pit mining operation measuring 1,100 feet wide by 2,000 feet long and had planned to mine for at least 20 years. The number of employees had been estimated at 50 to 150 with an annual payroll of six to seven million dollars.

The use of cyanide in mining was developed in Europe in 1878, but had not been used extensively in the United States until J.S. Cain, Bodie's benefactor, and A.J. McCone, a prominent mining and foundry developer in Virginia City, combined forces and decided such a system was made to order for the huge slag heaps left by the mines in Bodie. Cain and McCone were determined to salvage the gold they knew was left in those thousands of tons of mine tailings. They experimented in treating the tailings with cyanide of potassium, one of the most deadly poisons known to man.

Cain and McCone purchased most of the mine tailings in the Bodie area and hired a New Zealand metallurgist to build and operate one of the first cyanide plants in the United States. They paid him the then unheard of salary of $1,000 per month and with his assistance constructed Bodie's South End cyanide treatment plant. Cain later hired a brother-in-law, Lester E. Bell, as his assistant. When Bell learned the cyanide process he succeeded the New Zealand expert.

'Honest Old Lester' he was always called, and 'twas said no matter how much gold passed through his hands none of it ever stuck to his fingers. Three other plants were built in quick succession by Cain and McCone—the Bodie Tunnel Plant, the Victor and the Del Monte.

The farmers down the canyon and on into Nevada who were supplied with water from Bodie Creek, had previously put an injunction on the Bodie Mines, prohibiting them from letting any more tailings wash into the creek. The tailings had deposited a yellow coat of soil over their farming lands. Thereafter, the tailings, with their golden treasure, had to be banked up in Bodie. Little did the farmers dream that by this injunction they were stopping a golden flood from continuing to inundate their land, nor did they dream of the profit they would realize from the yellow coat which had already been deposited. Some time later Cain and McCone sent their cyanide men down to help the farmers build plants on their ranches (a small plant was not costly) and they worked the tailings for themselves.

Thus Bodie was given a shot in the arm as a result of the new cyanide process. A total of nine cyanide plants were built.

Galactic Resources staked mining claims on 20,000 acres of Federal Bureau of Land Management holdings surrounding Bodie, in addition to its initial patent claim for 550 acres over the bluff at a cost of another $350,000, according to Whitehead.

Galactic's future, and that of Bodie Consolidated Mining Co., ended rather abruptly in 1992, however, at Summitville, Colorado. For a period of two years, Galactic had operated an open pit gold mine under the firm name of "Summitville Consolidated Mining Co." During that period it had removed about $30 million in gold, but was faced with disaster when a spill of cyanide acid solution from its heap leach processing facility contaminated hundreds of acres of land and a 17-mile stretch of the Alamosa River system. The damage cost the Federal Environmental Protection Agency Super Fund (toxic cleanup fund) $170 million–about 10 per cent of the entire fund.[2]

Galactic was forced to file for Chapter 11 bankruptcy as a result of the spill, thus closing down its Bodie operations and bringing to an end any plans to mine gold and silver there.

Two similar disasters occurred elsewhere in the world following the Colorado spill. The first was in August, 1995 in Guyana, when masses of dead fish and pigs floated down the Essequibo River, the largest tributary in that South American nation. They were victims of a cyanide waste spill that also escaped from a gold mine operated by companies from Colorado and Canada. More than 325 million gallons of the toxic chemical solution also threatened public drinking water supplies as it flowed 50 miles downstream. International relief teams were rushed in and contained the cyanide in a holding pond near the mines.

The spill occurred at the Omai Gold Mines owned jointly by Cambior, Inc. of Montreal and Colorado and Goldstar Resources of Edmonton, Alberta. It first polluted the Omai River which continued on to flow into the Essequibo. Ironically the spill of cyanide-polluted water occurred close to the infamous Jonestown mass suicide/murder site where cult leader Jim Jones' members died–most from drinking a cyanide-laced soft drink. Another catastrophe involving cyanide.[3]

The second was a spill that occurred January 30, 2000, in what has been described as Europe's worst environmental disaster since Chernobyl, again involving gold mining operations. A cyanide spill from an overflowing dam at the Baia Mare Gold Mine owned by Esmeralda Exploration Co. of Perth, Australia, sent cyanide laden water into nearby streams. These flowed west into the Tisa River in neighboring Hungary and then on into Yugoslavia where the flow entered the Danube River. Cities down stream were forced to shut off pumps that normally delivered fresh drinking water and fish kills were reported along all the contaminated tributaries.[4]

Officials described the spill as comparable to Galactic's Colorado cyanide spill of 1992.[5]

Following the demise of Bodie Consolidated Mining Co., the State of California and the federal government entered into an agreement. In July, 1997, California authorized an expenditure of $3 million, supplemented by a federal authorization of $2 million. This paid for the patent rights to the 550 acres that was to have been Galactic's open pit mining operation at the edge of Bodie Historic State Park that originally cost Galactic almost $34.5 million, putting an end to the threat of mining on Bodie Bluff, and leaving the State of California with an estimated two billion dollars worth of gold and silver untouched in the ground as well as additional land for Bodie Park.[6]

The purchase of the 550 acres was in line with the State Park and Recreation Commission Bodie Historic State Park Resource Management Plan, General Development Plan and Environmental Impact Report established in 1979.

Bodie Park rangers already are leading guided tours up onto the bluff for visitors who wish to tour the old railroad depot and make pre-arranged plans with the ranger office.

When the authors visited Bodie Bluff with Whitehead in 1991 he stated the mining company was very excited about its mining proposal. "In our core sampling we've found a tremendous potential. We know that there is a potential gold recovery of up to three ounces per ton in the areas we've surveyed," he said, adding:

"Mining around Bodie since 1859 removed one and a quarter-million ounces of gold and 25 million ounces of silver, and yet the old timers missed the real heart of Bodie's mother lode, which," he maintained, "still lies untouched."

The geology of Bodie Bluff indicated three volcanic flows dating as far back as 11 to 12 million years, Whitehead explained. The south area, referred to as "Silver Hill" is generally dedicated to silver bearing ore, a blue-toned rock. The northerly area contains gold bearing ore and is a sandy, brown-colored rock. The two distinct areas were formed from an earthquake zone referred to as the Mono Fault.

When it was determined in 1878 that the two areas of gold and silver ore contained gold in amounts of up to eight ounces per ton, and silver of up to 20 ounces per ton, the "boom" began for Bodie!

Old Jim Cain, who bought up land in and around Bodie prior to 1900, as it came on the market, maintained until his dying day that much more gold lay deep in those Bodie mountains, just waiting for the miner's pick. Apparently he was correct, or at least his grandson, the late Walter Cain, believed he was. When Walter was offered millions for the property rights by Homestake, he decided to sell. He and others in the Cain family believed not only in the value of the precious metal in the Bodie area, but in the historical value of the town. The Cain family in 1962 entered into an agreement with the State of California to sell the entire town to be established as a state historic park. The sale was consummated for the sum of $88,100, although the Cains valued the property at $350,000. Walter had insisted that the family was completely up front involving the mining situation. He stated just prior to his death:

THE PIKA: This small, short-eared mammal related to both the rabbit and the elephant, frequents the Bodie Bluff area, along with sage grouse, mule deer, antelope and other animals. Bodie Consolidated Mining Company was pledged to leave them undisturbed in their exploratory efforts in the early 1990's. (Photo from a private collection)

"We certainly don't want anything detrimental to happen to Bodie because of the mining. We have been assured by Galactic that all the mining will be done on the other side of the hill, out of sight and sound from the park. In our agreement with the State when we sold the town of Bodie it was stipulated that someday mining might be resumed on our property up on the hill."

Although the Cains had visions of continued mining around Bodie, the State apparently does not and through the purchase of the Galactic patent lease, has successfully put an end to such a possibility.

During the period from 1989 through 1994, Galactic was preparing for its eventual open pit mining program just to the east of Bodie Bluff, all the while maintaining such a project would not be detrimental to the town of Bodie. The company was preparing to take its plans before the Mono County Board of Supervisors and to state and federal authorities for approval under the 1970 California Environmental Quality Act (CEQA) and the National Environmental Policy Act (NEPA) as part of the 200-plus steps necessary in the process of permit issuance procedures.

No mining can occur without input from the public and an independent, comprehensive study to determine the effect upon the environment.

The Save Bodie! Committee, formed to combat Galactic's plans, stated at the time Galactic was moving forward with its plans:

"A disturbing indication of Galactic's environmental attitude is contained in an investment research report prepared by Kitcat, Aitken & Company for distribution to prospective investors in Galactic....this report states that if a cyanide leach plant is not permitted in California, Galactic has a contingency plan whereby ore could be transported by conveyor across the Nevada state line where the environmental lobby is not so strong."[4]

Galactic Geologist Whitehead refuted this statement at the time: "That type of system would be economically unfeasible for the mining firm."

Whitehead might have been correct, but such was not the case for another California gold mining company that operated an open pit mine at the edge of Jamestown, California in the Tuolumne County area of the California Mother Lode, located many miles further from Nevada than is Bodie. One-hundred tons of gold-bearing ore was trucked daily for some 14 years on a 9-1/2 hour, 395-mile round trip from Jamestown to a cyanide processing plant at the old Buckskin Mine in eastern Douglas County, nine miles west of Yerington, Nevada.[5] The Sonora Mining Co. ran out of gold-bearing ore and closed in 1995.[6]

At the time Sonora Mining began its long-haul operation, a company official, Brent Chamberlan, said the operation was "strictly a matter of economics and timetables. The company would have preferred to process its ore at Jamestown but because the State of California requires a two-year permit process, it was more expedient to save time and process the ore in Nevada."[7]

Bodie Consolidated, in its arguments in favor of mining near Bodie, stated: "When Emil Billeb, director of the J.S. Cain Co. in the 1950s and son-in-law of its founder, finally convinced the State of California to acquire the historic townsite of Bodie, all parties involved in the 1967 property transfer agreed that mining would someday return to the district.

"The state thought a working mine would not be a detrimental influence to a park unit but rather would be complimentary and that both parties understood the Cain interests wanted to preserve their property rights."

Said the late Walter Cain at the time of the sale of the town to the State: "The land being sold was limited to existing townsite boundaries; the streets were even ceded to the county so that they would be kept open to traffic, to provide access to the company's mineral claims."

A brochure, distributed by Bodie Consolidated Mining Co. at the time it was doing its core drilling exploration, stated: "The State's Department of Natural Resources not only agreed to the co-existence of park and mining but felt a renewal of mining would actually enhance the visitor experience....In a 1959 analysis, parks division investigator Paul R. Meier surmised that a free-floating price of gold and modern cyanide mining methods would likely mean renewed mining at Bodie."

The brochure quoted Meier: "I doubt if an active mining operation would detract anything from Bodie as a park unit. In fact, it might even be a complimentary feature."

The company's brochure went on to say: "The Division apparently agreed with its investigator's report; the property was purchased from the Cain Company for about a fourth of its market value and the park became a reality. And with the price of gold now determined by the market place rather than government decree, once again it may be economical to mine in the Bodie Mining District, thereby fulfilling the prophesy of the original parks division investigators."

Galactic Resources was so confident in its proposal to mine the Bodie area that it staked mining claims on 20,000 acres of Federal Bureau of Land Management holdings surrounding Bodie, in addition to its initial 550 acres, at a cost of $350,000, and Whitehead stated in 1991 that Galactic "would be glad to present the old railroad depot to the state historic park. We wanted to work with the park in every way we could. We hoped visitors to Bodie would also visit our mining operations and we planned to establish a visitor center in the mining area."[8]

The mining experience the visitor to Bodie today sees is the experience of the yesteryears. Gold and silver mining in Bodie is now a thing of the past.

FOOTNOTES — CHAPTER 14

1. John Holmgren, "The Backroads of Nevada," an article in Motorland Magazine, May / June, 1989
2. Mark Hunter, reporter, Alamosa (Colorado) Valley Courier, an interview, August, 1994
3. San Francisco Chronicle, August 14, 1995
4. Ibid., February 12, 2000
5. Stockton Record (Stockton, CA) February 13, 2000
6. Ibid., February 15, 2000
7. Ibid., September 18, 1990
8. "The Bodie Bulletin," Bodie Consolidated Mining Co. Newsletter, Summer, 1990

BIBLIOGRAPHY

BOOKS, ARTICLES AND GOVERNMENT PUBLICATIONS

Barlow, Ronald S., The Vanishing American Outhouse, El Cajon, CA, Windmill Publishing Company, 1989.

Billeb, Emil W., Mining Camp Days, Las Vegas, NV, Nevada Publications, 1986.

Brochure, Bodie Historic State Park, Summer 1990, Vol. 2, No. 1, Bodie Consolidate Mining Co., Bridgeport, CA.

Brochure, Bodie Historic State Park, California State Department of Parks and Recreation, 1990.

Browne, J. Ross, A Trip to Bodie Bluff and the Dead Sea of the West (Mono Lake) in 1863, Golden, Colorado Outbooks, 1981.

Calhuon, Margaret, Pioneers of Mono Basin, Artemisia Press, Lee Vining, California

Cain, Ella M., The Story of Bodie, San Francisco, CA and Sonora, CA, Fearon Publishers and Mother Lode Press, 1956.

Carter, William, Ghost Towns of the West, Menlo Park, CA, Lane Magazine 7 Book Company, 1977.

Johnson, Russ and Anne, The Ghost town of Bodie, as reported in the Newspapers of the Day, Bishop, CA, Chalfant Press, 1977.

Le Conte, Joseph N., A Summer of Travel in the High Sierra, Preface by Ansel Adams; Lewis Osborne; Ashland, Oregon, 1972.

Le May, Delcie P., Bodie Bill. Delcie P. LeMay, publisher, 1965.

Loose, Warren, Bodie Bonanza, The True Story of a Flamboyant Past, Las Vegas, NV, Nevada Publications, 1979.

McDonald, Douglas, Bodie Boom Town—Gold Town, The Last of California's Old-Time Mining Camps, Las Vegas, NV, Nevada Publications.

McGrath, Roger D., Gunfighters, Highwaymen and Vigilantes, University of California Press, Berkeley, Los Angeles, London, 1984.

Moore, Barbara, Bodie Electrifies the World, From the Album Times and Tales of the Inyo-Mono, Bishop, CA, Chalfant Press, Vol. 1, No. 3, July 1988.

Motorland Magazine, (editors) Barron Hilton's Flying M., July ,1988.

Myrick, David F., Railroads of Nevada and Eastern California. Berkeley, CA, Howell-North Books, 1962.

O'Rourke, Everett V., The Highest School in California, Sacramento Corral of Westerners, Publication Number Two, 1972 Book No. 283 of 500 Copies.

Russell, Israel G., Quaternary History of Mono Valley, California. 1883.

"Save Bodie! Committee" Newsletter, April 8, 1989.

"Save Bodie! Committee" Newsletter. March 9, 1990
Sunset Magazine, (editors) Bodie, Quiet Ghost Stirring, Menlo Park, California, Lane Publishing Co., May, 1990.

"The Bodie Bulletin, " Summer, 1990, Vol. 2, No. 1, Bodie Consolidated Mining Co., Bridgeport, CA.

The Columbia-Viking Desk Encyclopedia, Second Edition 1960, Columbia University Press, New York, NY.

The Pony Express, An Old Ghost Town Stirs, by David Lavender, Placerville, CA, August, 1944.

Twain, Mark, Roughing It, Berkeley, Los Angeles, London, University of California Press, 1973.

Wedertz, Frank S., Bodie 1859—1900, Bishop, Ca, Chalfant Press, 1969.

Williams III, George, The Guide to Bodie and Eastern Sierra Historic Sites, Riverside, California, Tree by the River Publishers, 1981.

Rosa May: The Search for a Mining Camp Legend, Riverside, California, Tree by the River Publishing, 1984.

NEWSPAPER BIBLIOGRAPHY

Atlanta Century, Atlanta, GA

Bodie Chronicle

Bodie Daily Standard

Bodie Evening Miner

Bodie Standard News

Bridgeport Chronicle-Union, Bridgeport, CA

Bridgeport Chronicle-Union & Bodie Chronicle

Calaveras Enterprise, San Andreas, CA

Inyo Register, Bishop, CA

Los Angeles Times

Mammoth City Times, Mammoth City, CA

Minden / Gardnerville Record Courier, Minden, NV

Out West

Poughkeepsie Journal, Poughkeepsie, NY

Reno Gazette Journal, Reno, NV

Reno Weekly Gazette

Sacramento Bee, Sacramento, CA

San Francisco Chronicle

San Francisco Examiner-Chronicle

Stockton Record, Stockton, CA

The Pony Express, Placerville, CA

INDEX

A

B

F

Fahey, Pat – 39
Fair, Ellen – 131
Fairview – 106
Falkinham, Joseph J. – 29
Farnsworth, Joe – 34, 35, 36, 41, 42
Federal Bureau of Land Management – 166, 171
Ferguson, R.D. – 12, 13
firebug – 61, 63, 69
Friends of Bodie – 103
Fuller, Annie – 47

G

Galactic – 162, 163, 164, 166, 167, 169, 170, 171
Garfield, President James A. – 13, 14, 15, 16
Garraty, Pat – 9
Gianettoni, Martin – 27
Giant Powder Company – 140
Gilson Barber & Company – 71, 150, 156
Gilson, George – 71, 156
Godward, Bodie Bill – 59, 60, 61, 62, 63, 64, 65, 66, 67, 68, 69, 70, 71, 73
    Canary Jane – 61, 62
    Delcie Pearl Millslagle – 63, 64, 65, 66, 67, 68, 69, 70, 71, 74
    William Brewster – 72, 73
    William T. – 63, 64
Goldstar Resources – 166
Golden Gate National Cemetery – 65, 73
Graves, R.M. – 87
Gray, Mrs. Loretta – 65, 66, 133
Great Depression – 102
Green Creek Hydroelectric Plant – 48, 112, 113, 151
    Street – 22, 23, 24, 48
Gregory, Spence – 27
Groth, George – 70, 71
Guyana – 166

H

Hallidie, A.S. – 121, 148, 150, 151
Hamlin, Herb S. – 126
Hammond, Jack – 113
Hannibal, MO – 124
Harden, Roland – 110, 112, 116
Hardy, Harold – 110, 112, 116
Harlow, Jean – 69
Haslett, Ben – 17
   John – 17
Hawthorne, NV – 51, 106, 123, 158
Head, Mrs. – 96
heap-leach process – 11, 162, 164
Heffernan, Arthur – 33
Heif, Henry – 128
"Hell's Angels" – 68, 69
"Hell's Heroes" – 68, 69
Higbie, Calvin – 120, 125, 126
High Peak – 95, 96
Highton, Jack – 158
hippies – 98
Hitchell, David T. – 40
Hoffman, Julia – 131
Holmgren, John – 163
Holt, John – 62
Homestake Mining – 147, 164, 168
Hoover, Herbert – 68, 159
   Theodore – 68, 159, 160
hops – 2, 25, 143
horse snowshoes – 139
Howland, Robert W. – 17, 18
Hughes, Howard – 69, 163
Hunt, James – 15, 16
Huntington, W.B. – 91

R

S

U

Universal Benevolent Assn. For Unmarried persons – 144
Universal Studios – 68, 69
Upton, E.V. – 160
urn – 22

V

Vancouver, B.C. – 163
VanZandt, Dr. J.W. – 15
Vigilance Committee – 33, 34
Vincent, J.H. – 160
Virgin Avenue – 131
Virginia & Truckee Railroad – 85, 86
Virtue Street – 131
volcanic flows – 167

W

Walker –
   Lake – 51, 153, 158
   L.P. – 81, 82
   River – 51
Ward, H. – 80
Ward's Undertaking Parlor – 39, 46, 79
Warm Springs – 51
Warren, N.S. – 160
Washoe Pete – 129
Wasson, Joseph – 11, 15, 16, 17
Wassuc Mountains – 51
Watson, Jim – 14, 23, 25, 35, 40, 44, 52, 76, 79, 80, 85, 89, 96, 99, 100,
   105, 106, 107, 108, 109, 126, 129, 132, 133, 142, 145, 148, 155, 164
Webber's Blacksmith Shop – 38
Wedertz, Frank S. – 18, 19, 95, 131, 147, 151
Wells, Kirkpatrick – 13
Weir, Harry W. – 108, 110, 111, 112
Whitehead, Mark L. – 96, 97, 162, 164, 166, 167, 169, 171